THE BOOK OF LIFE

THE BOOK OF LIFE

---

with The Spirit of Truth:
Voice of Bridegroom

Daniel Timothy Bridegroom

To order additional copies of this book, contact:
Xlibris
844-714-8691
www.Xlibris.com
Orders@Xlibris.com
841090

How lonely sits the city that was full of people! How like a widow is she, who was great among the nation! The princess among the provinces has become a slave! (Lam. 1:1). She weeps bitterly in the night, her tears are on her checks; among all her lovers she has none to comfort her. All her friends have dealt treacherously with her, they have become her enemies. 2 Judah has gone into captivity, under affliction and hard servitude; she dwells among the nations, she finds no rest; all her persecutors overtake her in dire straits. 3 The roads to Zion mourn because no one comes to "The Set Feast." All her gates are desolate; her priests sigh, her virgins are afflicted; and she is in bitterness. 4

Her adversaries have become the master, her enemies prosper; for The Lord has afflicted her because of the multitude of her transgressions. Her children have gone into captivity before the enemy. 5 And from The Daughter of Zion all her splendor has departed. Her princes have become like deer that find no pasture, that flee without strength before the pursuer. 6 In the days of her affliction and roaming, Jerusalem remembers all her pleasant things that she had in the days of old. When her people fell into the hand of her enemy, with no one to help her, the adversaries saw her and mocked at her downfall. 7

Jerusalem has sinned gravely, therefore she has become vile. All who honored her despise her because they have seen her nakedness; yes, she sighs and turns away. 8 Her uncleanness is in her skirts; she did not consider her destiny; therefore her collapse was awesome; she had no comforter. "O Lord, behold my affliction, for the enemy is exalted!" 9

"I called for my lovers, but they deceived me; my priests and my elders breathed their last in the city, while they sought food to restore their life." 19 Your prophets have seen for you false and deceptive visions; they have not uncovered your iniquity, to bring back your captives, but have envisioned for you false prophesies and delusions (2:14). The Lord has done what He purposed; He has fulfilled His Word which He has commanded in days of old. He has thrown down and has not pitied, and He has caused an enemy to rejoice over you; He has exalted the horn of your adversaries. 17

Deliver me from my enemies, O my God; defend me from those who rise up against me (Ps. 59:1). Deliver me from the workers of iniquity, and save me from bloodthirsty men. 2 At evening they return, they growl like a dog, and go all around the city. 6 Indeed, they belch with their mouth: swords are in their lips; for they say, "Who hears?" 7

But You, O Lord, shall laugh at them; You shall have all the nations in derision. 8 I will wait for You, O You his Strength; for God is my defense. 9 My God of Mercy shall come to meet me; God shall let me see my desire on my enemies. 10 For You have been a shelter for me, a strong tower from the enemy (61:3). I will abide in Your tabernacle forever, I will trust in The Shelter of Your Wings. Selah 4 For You, O God, have heard "My Vows"; You have given me the heritage of those who fear Your Name. 5 For I will sing praise to Your Name forever, that I may daily perform My Vows. 8

O God, You are my God; early will I seek You; my soul thirst for You; my flesh longs for You in a dry and thirsty land where there is no water (63:1). So I have looked for You in the sanctuary to see Your Power, and Your Glory. 2 Because Your lovingkindness is better than life, my lips shall praise You. 3 My soul follows close behind You; Your "Right Hand" upholds me. 8 But the king shall rejoice in God; everyone who swears by Him shall glory; but the mouth of those who speak lies shall be stopped. 11

Praise is waiting for You, O God, in Zion; and to You "The Vow" shall be performed (65:1). O You who hears prayer, to You all flesh will come. 2 Blessed is the man You choose, and caused to approach You, that he may dwell in Your Courts. We shall be satisfied with The Goodness of Your House, of Your Holy Temple. 4 By awesome deeds in righteousness You will answer us, O God of our salvation, You who are the confidence of all the ends of the earth, and of the far-off seas; 5 Who established the mountains by His Strength, being clothed with power; 6 You who still the noise of the seas, the noise of their waves, and the tumult of the peoples. 7

Oh, bless our God, you peoples! And make The Voice of His Praise to be heard (66:8). Come and hear, all you who Fear God, and I will declare what He has done for my soul. 16 But certainly God has heard me; He has attended to "The Voice" of my prayer. 19 Sing to God, sing praises to His Name; extol Him who rides on the clouds, by His Name YAH, and rejoice before Him (68:4). Sing to God, you kingdoms of the earth; oh, sing praises to The Lord, Selah 32 To Him who rides on the heavens of heaven, which were of old! Indeed, He sends out "His Voice," "A Mighty Voice." 33

I will call upon The Lord, who is worthy to be praised; so shall I be saved from my enemies (2 Sam. 22:4). "When the waves of death surrounded me, the floods of ungodliness made me afraid." 5 The sorrows of Sheol surrounded me; the snares of death confronted me. 6 In my distress I called upon The Lord, and cried out to my God; He heard My Voice from His temple, and my cry entered His ears. 7 "Then the earth shook and trembled; the foundations of heaven quaked and were shaken, because He was angry." 8 Smoke went up from His nostrils, and devouring fire from His mouth; coals were kindled by it. 9

He bowed the heavens also, and came down with darkness under His feet. 10 He rode upon a cherub, and flew; and He was seen upon the wings of the wind. 11 The Lord thundered from heaven, and The Most High uttered "His Voice." 14 Then the channels of the sea were seen, the foundations of the world were uncovered, at The Rebuke of The Lord, at The Blast of The Breath of His nostrils. 16

As for God, "His Way" is perfect; The Word of The Lord is proven; He is a shield to all who trust in Him. 31 "The Lord Lives!" Blessed be my Rock! Let God be exalted, The Rock of My Salvation! 47 Therefore I will give thanks to You, O Lord, among the Gentiles, and sing praise to "Your Name." 50

For now they say, "We have no king, because we did not Fear The Lord." And as for a king, what will He do for us? (Hosea 10:3). You have plowed wickedness; you have reaped iniquity. You have eaten the fruit of lies, because you have trusted in your own way, in the multitude of your mighty men. 13 And The Sword shall slash in his cities, devour his districts, and consume them, because of their own counsels (11:6). My People are bent on backsliding from Me. Though they call to The Most High, none at all "Exalt Him." 7

I have also spoken by the prophets, and have multiplied visions; I have given symbols through the witness of the prophets (12:10). By a prophet The Lord brought Israel out of Egypt, and by a prophet He was preserved. 13 Now they sin more and more, and have made for themselves molded images, idols of their silver, according to their skill; all of it is the work of craftsmen. They say of them, "Let the men who sacrifice kiss the calves!" (13:2).

"O Israel, you are destroyed, but your help is from Me." 9 I will be your king; where is any other, that he may save you in all your cities? And your judges to whom you said, "Give me a king and princes"? 10 I gave you a king in My Anger, and took Him away in My Wrath. 11 O Israel, return to The Lord your God, for you have stumbled because of your iniquity (14:1). Who is wise? Let him understand these things. Who is prudent? Let him know them. For "The Ways of The Lord" are Right; The Righteous walk in them, but transgressors stumble in them. 9

For what "The Law" could not do in that it was weak through the flesh, God did by sending His Own Son in the likeness of sinful flesh, on account of sin: He condemned sin in the flesh (Rom. 8:3). That "The Righteous' requirement of The Law" might be fulfilled in us who do not walk according to the flesh but according to "The Spirit." 4 But to be carnally minded is death, but to be Spiritually Minded is life and peace. 6 And we know that all things work together for good to those who love God, to those who are called according to "His Purpose." 28

For with the heart one believes unto righteousness, and with the mouth confession is made unto salvation (10:10). And so all Israel will be saved, as it is written: "The Deliverer will come out of Zion, and He will turn away ungodliness from Jacob (11:26). For this is My Covenant with them, when I take away their sins." 27 Therefore whoever resists the authority resists The Ordinance of God, and those who resist will bring judgment on themselves (13:2). Therefore you must be subject, not only because of wrath but also for conscience's sake. 5

Blessed be The God and Father of our Lord Jesus Christ, who according to "His Abundant Mercy" has "Begotten Us Again" to "A Living Hope" through the resurrection of Jesus Christ from the dead (1 Pet. 1:3). To an inheritance incorruptible and undefiled and that does not fade away, reserved in heaven for you. 4 Who are kept by The Power of God through faith for salvation ready to be revealed in "The Last Time." 5 Of This Salvation the prophets have inquired and searched carefully, who prophesied of the grace that would come to you. 10

Therefore gird up the loins of your mind, be sober, and rest your hope fully upon the grace that is to be brought to you at The Revelation of Jesus Christ; 13 As obedient children, not conforming yourselves to the former lusts, as in your ignorance; 14 But as He who called you is holy, you also be holy in all you conduct. 15 And if you call on The Father, who without partiality judges according to each one's work, conduct yourselves throughout the time of your stay here in fear; 17 Knowing that you were not redeemed with corruptible things, like silver and gold, from your aimless conduct received by tradition from your fathers, 18

He indeed was foreordained before the foundation of the world, but was manifest in "These Last Times" for you. 20 Having been "Born Again," not of corruptible seed but incorruptible, through "The Word of God" which lives and abides forever. 23 But "The Word of Lord" endures forever. Now this is "The Word" which by "The Gospel" was preached to you. 25 So each of us shall give account of himself to God (Rom. 14:12).

"Give ear, O heavens, and I will speak; and hear, O earth, The Words of my mouth" (Deut. 32:1). Let my teaching drop as the rain, my speech distill as the dew, as raindrops on the tender herb, and as showers on the grass. 2 For I proclaim the Name of the Lord: ascribe greatness to our God. 3 He is the Rock, His Work is perfect; for all His Ways are justice, A God of Truth and without injustice; Righteous and Upright is He. 4

And He said: I will hide My Face from them, I will see what their end will be, for they are a perverse generation, children in whom is no faith. 20 They have provoked Me to jealousy by what is not God; they have moved Me to anger by their foolish idols. But I will provoke them to jealousy by those who are not a nation; I will move them to anger by a foolish nation. 21 For a fire is kindled in My anger, and shall burn to the lowest hell; it shall consume the earth with her increase, and set on fire the foundations of the mountains. 22

"I will heap disasters on them; I will send My arrows on them. 23 They shall be wasted with hunger, devoured by pestilence and bitter destruction; I will also send against them the teeth of the beasts, with the poison of serpents of the dust. 24 The Sword shall destroy outside; there shall be terror within for the young men and virgin, the nursing child with the man of grey hairs. 25 Vengeance is Mine, and recompense; their foot shall slip in 'Due Time'; for The Day of their calamity is at hand, and the things to come hasten upon them."35

"Behold, all souls are Mine; the soul of the father as well as the soul of the son is Mine; the soul who sins shall die" (Ezek. 18:4). But if a man is Just and does what is Lawful and Right; 5 If he has not eaten on the mountains, nor lifted up his eyes to idols of The House of Israel, nor defiled his neighbor's wife, nor approached a women during her impurity; 6 If he has not oppressed anyone, but has restored to the debtor his pledge, has robbed no one by violence, but has given his bread to the hungry and covered the naked with clothing; 7 If he has not exacted usury nor taken any increase, but has withdrawn his hand from iniquity and executed "True Judgment" between man and man; 8 If he has "Walked in My Statutes" and "Kept My Judgments Faithfully"—he is Just; he shall surely Live!" says The Lord God. 9

"Do I have any pleasure at all that the wicked should die?" says The Lord God, "and not that he should 'Turn from his ways and live'?" 23 "Therefore I will judge you, O House of Israel, every one according to his ways," says The Lord God. "Repent, and turn from all your transgressions, so that iniquity will not be your ruin. 30 "Cast away from you all the transgressions which you have committed, and get yourselves 'A New Heart and A New Spirit,' for why should you die, O House of Israel? 31 "For I have no pleasure in the death of one who dies," says The Lord God. "Therefore 'Turn' and 'Live'!" 32

Blessed is he whose transgression is forgiven, whose sin is covered (Ps. 32:1). Blessed is the man to whom The Lord does not impute iniquity, and in 'Whose Spirit' there is no deceit. 2 I will instruct you and teach you in "The Way" you should go; I will guide you with My Eye. 8 Be glad in The Lord and rejoice, you righteous; and shout for joy, all you "Upright in Heart"! 11 The counsel of The Lord stands forever, The Plans of His Heart to all generations (33:11).

Oh, magnify The Lord with me, and let us "Exalt His Name Together" (Ps. 34:3). The angel of The Lord encamps around those who Fear Him, and delivers them. 7 Come, you children, listen to me; I will teach you "The Fear of The Lord." 11 Keep your tongue from evil, and your lips from speaking deceit. 13 Depart from evil and do good; seek peace and pursue it. 14 The Lord is near to those who have a broken heart, and

"Saves" such as have a contrite spirit. 18 And my soul shall be joyful in The Lord; it shall rejoice in "His Salvation" (35:9).

Be silent in The Presence of The Lord God; for The Day of The Lord is at hand, for The Lord has prepared a sacrifice, He has invited His guests (Zeph. 1:7). "And it shall be, in The Day of The Lord's sacrifice, that I will punish the princes and the king's children, and all as are clothed with foreign apparel. 8 In The Same Day I will punish all those who leap over the threshold, who fills their masters' houses with violence and deceit." 9 "And there shall be on That Day," says The Lord, "The sound of a mournful cry from The Fish Gate, a wailing from The Second Quarter, and a loud crushing from the hills." 10 "I will bring distress upon men, and they shall walk like blind men, because they have sinned against The Lord; their blood shall be poured out like dust, and their flesh like refuse." 17 Neither their silver nor their gold shall be able to deliver them in The Day of The Lord's Wrath; but the whole land shall be devoured by the fire of His jealousy, for He will make speedy riddance of all those who dwell in the land. 16

For The House of Israel and The House of Judah have dealt very treacherously with Me, says The Lord (Jer. 5:11). They have lied about The Lord, and said, "It is not He. Neither will evil come upon us, nor shall we see Sword or Famine. 12 And the prophets become wind, for 'The Word' is not in them. Thus shall it be done to them." 13 "Therefore look! The Lord has put a lying spirit in the mouth of these prophets of yours, and The Lord has declared disaster against you" (2 Chron. 18:22).

But to the wicked God says: "What right have you to declare My Statues, or take My Covenant in your mouth" (Ps. 50:16). Seeing you hate instruction and cast 'My Words' behind you? 17 When you saw a thief, you consented with him, and have been a partaker with adulterers. 18 You sit and speak against your brother: you slander your own mother's son. 20 These things you have done, and I kept silent; you thought I was altogether like you; but I will 'Rebuke You,' and set them in order before your eyes."21

Jesus answered them, "Most assuredly, I say to you, whoever commits sin is a slave of sin (John 8:34). "I speak what I have seen with My Father, and you do what you have seen with your father." 38 "You do the deeds of your father." Then they said to Him, "We were not born of fornication; we have one Father—God." 41 Jesus said to them, "If God were your Father, you would love Me, for I proceeded forth and came from God; nor have I come of Myself, but He sent Me. 42 "Why do you not understand My speech? Because you are not able to listen to 'My Word.'"43

"You are of your father the devil, and the desire of your father you want to do. He was a murderer from the beginning, and does not 'Stand in The Truth,' because there is no Truth in him. When he speaks a lie, he speaks from his own resources, for he is a liar and the father of it." 44 "But because I tell 'The Truth,' you do not believe Me. 45 "Which of you convicts Me of sin? And if I tell 'The Truth,' why do you not believe Me?" 46 "He who is of God hears 'God's Words'; therefore you do not hear, because you are not of God." 47 "And I do not seek My Own glory; there is 'One' who seeks and judges." 50 "Most assuredly, I say to you, if anyone keeps 'My Word' he shall never see death." 51

"But I will deliver you in 'That Day,'" says The Lord, "and you shall not be given into the hand of the men whom you are afraid" (Jer. 39:17). "For I will surely deliver you, and you shall not fall by The Sword; but your 'Life' shall be as a prize to you, because you have put your trust in Me," says The Lord.'" 18 "Once I have sworn by My Holiness; I will not lie to David" (Ps. 89:35). "His seed shall endure forever, and His Throne as the sun before Me; 36 It shall be established forever like the moon, even like 'The Faithful Witness' in the sky." Selah. 37

What man can live and not see death? Can he deliver his Life from the power of the grave? Selah. 48 The days of our Life are seventy years; and if by reason of strength they are eighty years, yet their boast is only labor and sorrow; for it is soon cut off, and we fly away (Ps. 90:10). Surely He shall deliver you from the snare of the fowler and from the perilous pestilence (91:3). He shall cover you with His feathers, and under His wings you shall take refuge, "His Truth" shall be your "Shield and Buckler." 4 You shall not be afraid of the terror by night, nor of the arrow that flies by day, 5 Nor of the pestilence that walk in darkness, nor of the destruction that lays waste at noonday. 6

A thousand may fall at your side, and ten thousand at your right hand; but it shall not come to you. 7 Only with your eyes shall you look, and see "the reward of the wicked." 8 Because you have made The Lord, who is my refuge, even The Most High, your dwelling place. 9 No evil shall befall you, nor shall any plague come near your dwelling. 10 For He shall give His angels charge over you, to keep you in all your ways. 11

"For 'The Bread of God' is He who comes down from heaven and gives Life to the world" (John 6:33). And Jesus said to them, "I Am 'The Bread of Life.' He who comes to Me shall never hunger, and he who believes shall never thirst. 35 "But I said to you that you have seen Me and yet you do not believe. 36 The world cannot hate you, but it hates Me because I testify of it that its works are evil (7:7). "If anyone wills to do His Will, he shall know concerning 'The Doctrine,' whether it is from God or whether I speak on My own authority." 17 "Do not judge according to appearance, but judge with 'Righteous Judgment.'" (7:24).

"You shall not add to 'The Word' which I commanded you, nor take from it, that you may keep The Commandments of The Lord your God which I commanded you" (Deut. 4:2). "Therefore be careful to observe them; for this is your Wisdom and your Understanding in the sight of the peoples who will hear all these statues, and say, 'Surely this great nation is a Wise and Understanding people.'" 6 "Only take heed to yourself, and diligently keep yourself, lest you forget the things which your eyes have seen, and lest they depart from your heart all the days of your 'Life.' And teach them to your children and your grandchildren." 9 "But from there you 'Will Seek' The Lord your God, and you 'Will Find' Him if 'You Seek Him' with all your heart and with all your soul." 29

"When you are in distress, and all these things come upon you in 'The Latter Days,' when 'You Turn' to The Lord your God and obey 'His Voice' 30 (For The Lord your God is 'A Merciful God') He will not forsake you nor destroy you, nor forget 'The Covenant' of your fathers which He swore to them." 31 "Therefore know 'This Day,' and consider in your heart, that The Lord Himself is God in heaven above and on the earth beneath; 'There Is No Other.'" 39

As it is written in the Prophets: "Behold, I send My Messenger before Your Face, who will prepare 'Your Way' before you" (Mark 1:2). "The Voice of one crying in the wilderness; 'Prepare 'The Way of The Lord': make 'His Paths' straight.'" 3 And Saying, "The Time is Fulfilled, and The Kingdom of God is at hand. Repent, and believe in The Gospel." 15 And in this confidence I intended to come to you before, that you might have a second benefit" (2 Cor. 1:15). "For to 'This End' I also wrote, that I might put you to the test, whether you are obedient in all things" (2:9).

"Now therefore," He said, "put away the foreign gods which are among you, and incline you heart to The Lord God of Israel" (Josh. 24:23). But "'The End' of all things is at hand; therefore be serious and watchful in your prayers" (1 Pet. 4:7). Beloved, do not think it strange 'The Fiery Trial' which is to try you, as though some strange thing happened to you; 12 But rejoice to the extent that you partake of Christ's sufferings, that when 'His Glory is revealed,' you may also be glad with exceeding joy. 13 Now "If the righteous one is scarcely saved, where will the ungodly and the sinners appear?" 18

"For there is nothing covered that will not be revealed, nor hidden that will not be known" (Luke 12:2). "Hypocrites! You can discern the face of the sky and of the earth, but how is it you do not discern 'This Time'?" 56 "Strive to enter through the narrow gate, for many I say to you, will seek to enter and will not be able" (13:24). "See! Your house is left to you desolate; and assuredly, I say to you, you shall not see Me until 'The Time' comes when you say, 'Blessed is He who comes in The Name of The Lord!'" 35 "He who rejects Me and does not receive 'My Words, has that which judges him—'The Word' that I have spoken will judge him in 'The Last Day'" (John 12:48). "For I have not spoken on My own authority: but The Father who sent Me gave Me a command, what I should say and what I should speak." 49 "And I know that His Command is 'Everlasting Life.' Therefore, whatever I speak, just as The Father has told Me, so I speak." 50

"Behold, My eye has seen all this, My ear has heard and understood it" (Job 13:1). What you know, I also know; I am not inferior to you. 2 But I would speak to The Almighty, and I desire to reason with God. 3

But you forgers of lies, you are all worthless physicians. 4 Oh, that you would be silent, and it would be your wisdom! 5 Will it be well when He searches you out? Or can you mock Him as one who mocks a man? 9 "Hold your peace with Me, and let Me speak, then let come on Me what may!" 13

But I am a worm, and no man; a reproach of men, and despised by the people (Ps. 22:6). All those who see Me ridicule Me; they shoot out the lip, they shake the head, saying, 7 "He trusted in The Lord, let Him rescue Him; let Him deliver Him, since He delights in Him!" 8 For dogs have surrounded Me; the congregation of the wicked has enclosed Me. They pierced My hands and My feet; 16 They divide My garments among them, and for My clothing they cast lots. 18

Who may ascend into The Hill of The Lord? Or who may stand in His Holy Place? (Ps. 24:3). He who has clean hands and a pure heart, who has not lifted up his soul to an idol, nor sworn deceitfully. 4 Good and Upright is The Lord; therefore He teaches sinners in "The Way" (25:8). Who is the man that fears The Lord? Him shall He teach in 'The Way' He chooses. 12 Into Your Hand I commit My Spirit; You have redeemed Me, O Lord God of Truth (31:5). The Counsel of The Lord stands forever, The Plans of His Heart to all generations (33:11).

"All things have been delivered to Me by My Father, and no one knows who The Son is except The Father, and who The Father is except The Son, and the one to whom The Son wills to 'Reveal Him.'" (Luke 10:22). And Jesus said to them, "Can the friends of 'The Bridegroom' mourn as long as 'The Bridegroom' is with them? But 'The Days' will come when 'The Bridegroom' will be taken away from them, and then they will fast" (Matt. 9:15). "Behold! My servant whom I have chosen, My Beloved in whom 'My Soul' is well pleased! I will put 'My Spirit' upon Him, and He will 'Will Declare' justice to the Gentiles" (Matt. 12:18). And in His Name Gentiles will trust. 21

"Therefore I say to you, every sin and blasphemy will be forgiven men, but the blasphemy against 'The Spirit' will not be forgiven men" (Matt. 12:31). "For by your words you will be justified, and by your words you will be condemned." 37 "For whoever does 'The Will' of My Father in heaven is My brother and sister and mother." 50 "When 'The Son of Man' comes in His Glory, and all The Holy Angels with Him, then He will sit on The Throne of His Glory" (Matt. 25:31). "All nations will be gathered before Him, and He will separate them one from another, as a shepherd divides his sheep from the goats." 32 "Then 'The King' will say to those on His Right Hand, 'Come, you blessed of My Father, inherit 'The Kingdom' prepared for you from The Foundation of the world:'"34

O Jerusalem, wash your heart from wickedness, that you may be saved. How long will your evil thoughts lodge within you? (Jer. 4:14). "Make mention to the nations, yes, proclaim against Jerusalem, that watchers come from a far country and raise their voice against the cities of Judah. 16 Like keepers of a field they are against her all around, because she has been rebellious against Me," says The Lord. 17 "Sigh therefore, son of man, with a breaking heart, and sigh with bitterness before their eyes" (Ezek. 21:6).

"Look, the princes of Israel: each one has used his power to shed blood" (Ezek. 22:6). "In you they have made light of father and mother; in your midst they have oppressed the stranger; in you they have mistreated the fatherless and the widow." 7 "You have despised My Holy Things and profaned My Sabbaths.: 8 For in six days The Lord made the heavens and the earth, the sea, and all that is in them, and rested The Seventh

Day. Therefore The Lord blessed The Sabbath Day and hallowed it (Exod. 20:11).

It is time for You to act, O Lord, for they have regarded Your Law as void (Ps. 119:126). They draw near who follow after wickedness; they are far from Your Law. 150 I see the treacherous, and am disgusted, because they do not keep Your Word. 158 The entirely of Your Word is "Truth," and every one of Your Righteous Judgments endures forever. 160 Great Peace have those who love Your Law, and nothing causes them to stumble. 165

Have mercy on us, O Lord, have mercy on us! For we are exceedingly filled with contempt (Ps. 123:3). Our soul is exceedingly filled with the scorn of those who are at ease, with the contempt of the proud. 4 The idols of the nations are silver and gold, the work of men's hands (Ps. 135:15). Let burning coals fall upon them; let them be cast into the fire, into deep pits, that they rise not up again (Ps. 140:10).

Set a guard, O Lord, over My Mouth; keep watch over the door of My Lips (Ps. 141:3). Do not incline My Heart to any evil thing, to practice wicked works with men who work iniquity; and do not let me eat of their delicacies. 4 Let the righteous strike me; it shall be as kindness. And let him rebuke; it shall be as excellent oil; let My Head not refuse it. For still My Prayer is against the deeds of the wicked. 5 Their judges are overthrown by the sides of the cliff, and they hear My Words, for they are sweet. 6 Keep Me from the snares they have laid upon Me, and from the traps of the workers of iniquity. 9 Let the wicked fall into their own nets, while I escape safely. 10

Therefore My Spirit is overwhelmed within Me; My Heart within Me is distressed (Ps. 143:4). I remember the days of old; I meditate on all

Your Works; I muse on The Work of Your Hands. 5 I spread out My Hands to You; My Soul longs for You like a thirsty land. Selah 6 Cause Me to hear Your Lovingkindness in the morning, for in You do I trust; cause Me to know "The Way" in which I should walk, for I lift up My Soul to You. 8 Teach Me to do Your Will, for You are My God; Your Spirit is good. Lead Me in "The Land of Uprightness." 10

"When I would have healed Israel, then the iniquity of Ephraim was uncovered, and the wickedness of Samaria. For they have committed fraud; a thief comes in; a band of robbers take spoil outside" (Hosea 7:1). "They do not consider in their hearts that I remember all their wickedness; now their own deeds have surrounded them; they are before My Face. 2 And the pride of Israel testifies to His Face, but they do not 'Return' to The Lord their God, nor 'Seek Him' for all this. 10 Woe to them, for they have fled from Me! Destruction to them, because they have transgressed against Me! Though I redeemed them, yet they have spoken lies against Me." 13

"Because Ephraim has made many altars for sin, they have become for him 'altars for sinning'" (Hosea 8:11). Do not rejoice, O Israel, with joy like other peoples, for you have played the harlot against your God. You have made love for hire on every threshing floor (9:1). What will you do in The Appointed Day, and in The Day of The Feast of The Lord? 5 Sow for yourselves Righteousness; reap in mercy; break up your fallow ground, for "It is Time" to Seek The Lord, till "He Comes" and rains Righteousness on you. 12 And "The Sword" shall slash in his cities, devour his districts, and consume them, because of their own counsels (11:6).

"Ephraim feeds on the wind, and pursues the east wind; He daily increases lies and desolation. Also they make a covenant with the

Assyrians, and oil is carried to Egypt" (12:1). "The Lord also brings a charge against Judah, and will punish Jacob according to his ways; according to his deeds He will recompense him." 2 O Israel, Return to The Lord your God, for you have stumbled because of your iniquity (14:1).

Whoever causes The Upright to go astray in an evil way, he himself will fall into his own pit; but the blameless will inherit good (Prov. 28:10). A ruler who lacks understanding is a great oppressor, but he who hates covetousness will prolong his days. 16 Whoever walks blamelessly will be saved, but he who is perverse in his ways will suddenly fall. 18 When the wicked arise, men hide themselves; but when they perish, the righteous increase. 28 When The Righteous are in authority, the people rejoice; but when a wicked man rules, the people groan (29:2). If a ruler pays attention to lies, all his servants become wicked. 12 Whoever is a partner with a thief hates his own life; he swears to tell The Truth, but reveals nothing. 24

Now therefore, behold, The Lord brings up over them the waters of The River, strong and mighty—the king of Assyria and all his glory; he will go up over all his channels and go up over all his banks (Isa. 8:7). He will pass through Judah, he will overflow and pass over, he will reach up to the neck; and The Stretching Out of His Wings will fill the breadth of Your Land, O Immanuel. 8 Take counsel together, but it will come to nothing; "Speak The Word," but it will not stand, "For God is with Us." 10

"Woe to those who decree unrighteous decrees, who write misfortune, which they have prescribed" (Isa. 10:1). To rob the needy of justice, and to take what is Right from the poor of My People, that widows may be their prey, and that they may rob the fatherless." 2 "Woe to Assyria, the rod of My Anger and the staff in whose hand is My Indignation. 5 Therefore it shall come to pass, when The Lord has performed all His Work on Mount Zion and on Jerusalem, that He will say, "I will punish the fruit of the arrogant heart of the king of Assyria, and the glory of his haughty looks." 12

Therefore The Lord, The Lord of hosts, will send leanness among his fat ones; and under His Glory He will kindle a burning like the burning of a fire. 16 So The Light of Israel will be for a fire, and "His Holy One" for a flame; it will burn and devour his thorns and his briers in "One Day." 17 And it shall come to pass in "That Day" that the remnant of Israel, and such as have escaped of The House of Jacob, will "Never Again" depend on him who defeated them, but will depend on "The Lord, The Holy One of Israel," in ""Truth." 20

"Thus says The Lord God: 'Because the Philistines dealt vengefully and took vengeance with a spiteful heart, to destroy because of the old hatred'" (Ezek. 25:15). "I will execute 'Great Vengeance' on them with furious rebukes; and they shall know that 'I Am The Lord, when I lay My vengeance upon them.'" 17 "'I will make you a terror, and you shall be no more; though you are sought for, you will never be found again,' says The Lord God" (26:21).

When The Lord brought back The Captivity of Zion, we were like those who dream (Ps. 126:1). Then our mouth was filled with laughter, our tongue with singing. Then they said among the nations, "The Lord has done great things for them." 2 The Lord has done great things for us, and we are glad. 3 Bring back our captivity, O Lord, as the streams in the south. 4 "Flee, save your lives! And be like the juniper in the wilderness" (Jer. 48:6).

The Lord is My Strength and Song, and He has become My Salvation; He is My God, and I will praise Him; My father's God, and I will Exalt Him (Exod. 15:2). The Lord is a man of war; The Lord is His Name. 3 And in 'The Greatness of Your Excellence' You have overthrown those who rose against You; You sent forth Your Wrath; it consumed them like stubble. 7 "Who is like You, O Lord, among the gods? Who is like You, glorious in holiness, fearful in praises, doing wonders?" 11 The people will hear and be afraid; sorrow will take hold of the inhabitants of Philistia. 14 Fear and dread will fall on them; by The Greatness of Your Arm they will be as still as a stone, till Your People pass over, O Lord, till The People whom You have purchased. 16 You will "Bring Them" in and "Plant Them" in "The Mountain of Your Inheritance," in "The Place," O Lord, which You Have Made for Your Own Dwelling, "The Sanctuary," O Lord, which Your Hands have established. 17 "The Lord shall reign forever and ever." 18

"I will tell you, hear me; what I have seen I will declare" (Job 15:17). What the wise men have told, not hiding anything received from their fathers, 18 To whom alone the land was given, and no alien passed among them: 19 The wicked man writhes with pain all his days, and the number of years is hidden from the oppressor. 20 Dreadful sounds are in his ears; in prosperity the destroyer comes upon him. 21 Trouble and anguish make him afraid; they overpower him, like a king ready for battle. 24 For he stretches out his hand against God, and acts defiantly against The Almighty, 25 Let him not trust in futile things, deceiving himself, for futility will be his reward. 31 For the company of hypocrites will be barren, and fire will consume the tents of bribery. 34

Are not mockers with me? And does not my eye dwell on their provocation? (Job 17:2). Yet the righteous will hold to his way, and he who has clean hands will be stronger and stronger. 9 Why are we counted as beasts, and regarded as stupid in your sight? (18:3). This is "The History of The Heavens and The Earth" when they were created, in "The Day" that The Lord God made the earth and the heavens (Gen. 2:4). And The Lord God formed man of the dust of the ground, and breathed into his nostrils "The Breath of Life"; and man became a living being. 7 You are "of God," little children, and have overcome them, because He who is in you is greater than he who is in the world (1 John 4:4). We are "of God." He who knows God hear us; he who is not of God does not hear us. By this we know "The Spirit of Truth" and the spirit of error. 6a

"And now I stand and am judged for The Hope of The Promise made by God to our fathers" (Acts 26:6). "Why should it be thought incredible by you that God raises the dead?" 8 "But rise and stand on your feet; for I have appeared to you for this purpose, to make you a minister and a witness both of the things which you have seen and of things which I will yet reveal to you." 16 "I will deliver you from the Jewish people, as well as from the Gentiles, to whom now 'I Send You.'" 17 "To open their eyes, in order to turn them from darkness to light, and the power of Satan to God, that they may receive forgiveness of sins and an inheritance among those who are sanctified by faith in Me." 18 "Therefore, having obtained help from God, to This Day I Stand, witnessing both to small and great, saying no other things than those which the prophets and Moses said would come." 22 "That 'The Christ' would suffer, and He would be 'The First' to rise from the dead, and would 'Proclaim Light' to the Jewish people and to the Gentiles." 23

"Blessed is The Lord God of Israel, for He has visited and redeemed His People" (Luke 1:68) "And has raised up 'A Horn of Salvation' for us in The House of His Servant David, 69 As He spoke by The Mouth of His holy prophets, who have been since the world began, 70 That we should be Saved from our enemies and from the hand of all who hate us, 71 To perform the mercy promised to our fathers, and to remember 'His Holy Covenant,' 72 'The Oath' which He swore to our father Abraham: 73 To grant us that we, being delivered from the hand of our enemies, might serve Him without fear, 74 In holiness and righteousness before Him all the days of our Life." 75

For many walk, of whom I have told you often, and now tell you even weeping, that they are the enemies of "The Cross of Christ" (Phil. 3:18). Whose end is destruction, whose god is their belly, and whose glory is in their shame—who set their mind on earthly things. 19 He is proud, knowing nothing, but is obsessed with disputes and arguments over words, from which come envy, strife, reviling, evil suspicions (1 Tim. 6:4). But those who desire to be rich fall into temptation and a snare, and into many foolish and harmful lusts which drown men in destruction and perdition. 9

But if you bite and devour one another, beware lest you be consumed by one another! (Gal. 5:15). And let us not grow weary while doing good, for "In Due Season" we shall reap if we do not lose heart (6:9). But God forbid that I should boast except in The Cross of our Lord Jesus Christ, by whom the world has been crucified to Me, and I to the world. 14 For now on let no one trouble Me, for I bear in My Body "The Marks of The Lord Jesus" 17.

But there were also false prophets among the people, even as there will be false teachers among you, who will secretly bring in destructive heresies, even denying The Lord who bought them, and bring on themselves swift destruction (2 Pet. 2:1). And many will follow their destructive ways, because of whom "The Way of Truth" will be blasphemed. 2 By covetousness they will exploit you with deceptive words; for a long time their judgment has been idle, and their destruction does not slumber. 3 For if, after they have escaped the pollutions of the world through The Knowledge of The Lord and Savior Jesus Christ, they are again entangled in them and overcome, "The Latter End" is worse for them than the beginning. 20

But this people has a defiant and rebellious heart; "They Have Revolted and Departed" (Jer. 5:23). They do not say in their heart, "Let us now fear The Lord our God, who gives rain, both the former and The Latter, in its season. He reserves for us The Appointed Weeks of The Harvest." 24 You iniquities have turn these things away, and your sins withheld good from you. 25 They have grown fat, they are sleek; yes, they surpass the deeds of the wicked; they do not plead "The Cause," the cause of the fatherless; yet they prosper, and the right of the needy they do not defend. 28 An astonishing and horrible thing has been committed in the land: 30 The prophets prophesy falsely, and the priest rule by their own power; and My People love to have it so. "But what will you do in The End?" 31

Thus says The Lord: "Stand in The Ways and See, and ask for the old paths, where 'The Good Way' is, and walk in it; then you will find rest for your souls." But they said, 'We will not walk in it'" (6:16). "Also, I set watchmen over you, saying, 'Listen to The Sound of The Trumpet!' But they said, 'We will not listen.' 17 Hear O earth! Behold, I will certainly bring calamity on this people—the fruit of their thoughts, because they have not heeded 'My Words nor My Law,' but rejected it. 19 Listen! The Voice, the cry of The Daughter of My People from a far country": "Is not The Lord in Zion? Is not Her King in Her?" "Why have they provoked Me to anger with their carved images—with foreign idols?" (8:19).

But The Lord is The True God; He is The Living God and The Everlasting King. At His Wrath the earth will tremble, and the nations will not be able to endure His Indignation (Jer. 10:10). When He utters His Voice, there is a multitude of waters in the heavens: "And He causes the vapors to ascend from the ends of the earth. He makes lightning for the rain, He brings the wind out of His treasuries." 13 "For The Lord of hosts, who planted you, has pronounced doom against you for the evil of The House of Israel and of The House of Judah, which they have done against themselves to provoke Me to anger in offering incense to Baal" (11:17). Now The Lord gave Me knowledge of it, and I know it; for You showed me their doings. 18 But, O Lord of hosts, you who judge righteously, Testing the mind and the heart, let Me see Our vengeance on them, for to You I have revealed "My Cause." 20

Righteous are You, O Lord, when I plead with You; yet let me talk with You about Your Judgments. Why does the way of the wicked prosper? Why are those happy who deal so treacherously? (Jer. 12:1). You have planted them, yes, they have taken root; they grow, yes, they bear fruit. You are near in their mouth, but far from their mind. 2 But You, O Lord, know me; you have seen me, and You have tested my heart toward You. Pull them out like sheep for the slaughter, and prepare them for "The Day of Slaughter." 3 How long will the land mourn, and the herbs of every field wither? The beasts and birds are consumed, for the wickedness of those who dwell there, because they said, "He will not see our final end." 4 They have made it desolate; desolate, it mourns to Me; the whole land is made desolate, because no one takes it to heart. 11

Hear and give ear: do not be proud, for The Lord has spoken (13:15). But if you will not hear, My soul will weep in secret for your pride; My eye will weep bitterly and run down with tears, because The Lord's Flock has been taken captive. 17 And if you say in your heart, "Why have these things come upon me?" For the greatness of you iniquities your skirt has been uncovered, your heels made bare. 22 Can the Ethiopian change his skin or the leopard its spots? Then may you also do good who are accustomed to do evil. 23 This is your lot, the portion of your measure from Me, says The Lord, "Because you have forgotten Me and trusted in falsehood." 25

Woe to her who is rebellious and polluted, to the oppressing city! (Zeph. 3:1). She has not obeyed His Voice, she has not received correction; she has not trusted in The Lord, she has not drawn near to her God. 2 I said, "Surely you will Fear Me, you will receive instruction"—so that her dwelling would not be cut off, despite everything for which I punished her. But they rose early and corrupted all their deeds. 7

Therefore you are inexcusable, O man, whoever you are who judge, for in whatever you judge another you condemn yourself; for you who judge practice the same things (Rom. 2:1). But we know that "The Judgment of God" is according to Truth against those who practice the same things. 2 And do you think this, O man, you who judge those practicing such things, and doing the same, that you will escape "The Judgment of God"? 3 Or do you despise The Riches of His Goodness, forbearance, and longsuffering, not knowing that The Goodness of God leads you to repentance? 4 But in accordance with your hardness and your impenitent heart you are treasuring up for yourself wrath in The Day of Wrath and Revelation of The Righteous Judgment of God, 5 Who "will render to each one according to his deeds"? 6

Do not be unequally yoked together with unbelievers, For what fellowship has righteousness with lawlessness? And what communion has Light with darkness? (2 Cor. 6:14). And what accord has Christ with Belial? Or what part has a believer with an unbeliever? 15 And what agreement has The Temple of God with idols? For you are The Temple of The Living God, As God has said: "I will dwell in them and walk among them, I will be their God, and they shall be My People." 16 Therefore "Come out from among them and be separate," says The Lord. Do not touch what is unclean, and I will receive you. 17 "I will be a Father to you, and you shall be My sons and daughters, says The Lord Almighty." 18

"For I will 'Restore' health to you and heal you from your wounds, says The Lord, 'Because they called you an outcast saying: "This is Zion; no one seeks her""" (Jer. 30:17). "Thus says The Lord: 'Behold, I will bring back the captivity of Jacob's tents, and have mercy on his dwelling places; the city shall be built on its own mound, and the palace shall remain according to its own plan. 18 Then out of them shall proceed thanksgiving and the voice of them that make merry; I will multiply them, and they shall not diminish; I will also glorify them, and they shall not be small. 19 Their children shall be as before, and their congregation shall be establish before Me; and I will punish all who oppress them. 20 Their nobles shall be from among them, and their governor shall come from their midst; then I will cause him to draw near, and he shall approach Me; for who is this who pledges his heart to approach Me?' says The Lord." 21

"But I said to their children in the wilderness, 'Do not walk in the statues of your fathers, nor observe their judgments, nor defile yourselves with their idols'" (Ezek. 20:18). "I am The Lord your God: Walk in My Statutes, keep My Judgments, and do them; 19 Hallow My Sabbaths, and they will be a sign between Me and you, that you may know that I am The Lord your God." 20 "What you have in your mind shall never be, when you say, 'We will be like the Gentiles, like the families in other countries, serving wood and stone.'" 32 "I will purge the rebels from among you, and those who transgress against Me; I will bring them out of the country where they dwell, but they shall not enter the land of Israel. Then you will know that I am The Lord." 38

I beheld the earth, and indeed it was without form, and void; and the heavens, they had no light (Jer. 4:23). I beheld the mountains, and indeed they trembled, and all the hills moved back and forth. 24 I beheld, and indeed there was no man, and all the birds of the heavens had fled. 25 I beheld, and indeed the fruitful land was a wilderness, and all its cities were broken down at The Presence of The Lord, by His Fierce Anger. 26 "And when you are plundered, what will you do? Though you clothe yourself with crimson, though you adorn yourself with ornaments of gold, though you enlarge your eyes with paint, in vain will you make yourself fair; your lovers will despise you; they will seek your Life." 30

"And now, because you have done all these works," says The Lord, "and I spoke to you, rising up early and speaking, but you did not hear, and I called you, but you did not answer" (Jer. 7:13). "Since the day that your fathers came out of the land Egypt until 'This Day,' I have sent to you all My servants the prophets, daily rising up early and sending them. 25 Yet they did not obey Me or incline their ear, but stiffened their neck. They did worse than their fathers." 26

These six things The Lord hates, yes, seven are an abomination to Him (Prov. 6:16). A proud look, a lying tongue, hands that shed innocent blood, 17 A heart that devises wicked plans, feet that are swift in running to evil, 16 A false witness who speak lies, and one who sows discord among brethren. 19

For Jerusalem stumbled, and Judah is fallen, because their tongue and their doings are against The Lord, to provoke The Eyes of His Glory (Isa. 3:8). Just as it is written: "God has given them a spirit of stupor, eyes that should not see and ears that they should not hear, to This Very Day" (Rom. 11:8). Israel empties his vine; he brings forth fruit for himself. According to the multitude of his fruit he has increased altars; according to the bounty of his land they have embellished his sacred pillars (Hosea 10:1). Their heart is divided; now they are held guilty. He will break down their altars; He will ruin their sacred pillars. 2

"When Israel was a child, I loved him, and out of Egypt I called My son" (Hosea 11:1). As they called them, so they went from them: they sacrificed to Baals, and burned incense to carved images. 2 "I taught Ephraim to walk, taking them by their arms; but they did not know that I healed them." 3 I drew them with gentle cords, with Bands of Love, and I was to them as those who take the yoke from their neck. I stooped and fed them. 4 "Ephraim feeds on the wind, and pursues the east wind; He daily increases lies and desolation. Also they made a covenant with the Assyrians, and oil is carried to Egypt" (12:1).

When Ephraim spoke, trembling, he exalted himself in Israel; but when he offended through Baal worship, he died (Hosea 13:1). "Yet I Am The Lord your God ever since the land of Egypt, and you shall know no God but Me; for there is no Savior besides Me." 4 "And I will show wonders in the heavens and in the earth: blood and fire and pillars of smoke" (Joel 2:30). The sun shall be turned into darkness, and the moon into blood, before The Coming of The Great and Awesome Day of The Lord. 31 And it shall come to pass that whoever calls on The Name of The Lord shall be saved. For in Mount Zion and in Jerusalem there shall be Deliverance, as The Lord has said, among The Remnant Whom The Lord Calls. 32

To everything there is a season, a time for every purpose under heaven (Eccles. 3:1). A time to be born, and a time to die: a time to plant, and a time to pluck what is planted; 2 A time to kill, and a time to heal; a time to break down, and a time to build up; 3 A time to weep, and a time to laugh; a time to mourn, and a time to dance: 4 A time to cast away stones; and a time to gather stones; a time to embrace, and a time to refrain from embracing; 5 A time to gain, and a time to lose; a time to keep, and a time to throw away; 6 A time to tear, and a time to sew; a time to keep silence, and a time to speak; 7 A time to love, and a time to hate; a time of war, and a time of peace. 8

Moreover I saw under the sun; In The Place of Judgment, wickedness was there; and in The Place of Righteousness, iniquity was there. 17 I said in my heart, "God shall judge the righteous and the wicked, and there is A Time there for every purpose and for every work." 18 Do not say, "Why were the former days better than these?" For you do not inquire wisely concerning This (Eccles. 7:10). "For there is not a just man on earth who does good and does not sin. 20 For many times, also, your own heart has known that even you have cursed others. 22 All This I have proven 'by wisdom.' I said, 'I will be wise'; but it was far from me." 23

Who is like a wise man? And who knows The Interpretation of A Thing? A man's wisdom makes his face to shine, and the sternness of his face is changed (Eccles. 8:1). For man also does not know his time: like a fish taken in a cruel net, like birds caught in a snare, so the sons of men are snared in an evil time, when it falls suddenly upon them (9:12). Words of The Wise, spoken quietly, should be heard rather than the shout of a ruler of fools. 17

The kings of the earth, and all the inhabitants of the world, would not of believed that the adversary and the enemy could enter the gates of Jerusalem (Lam. 4:12). Because of the sins of her prophets and the iniquities of her priests, who shed in her midst the blood of the just. 13 We pay for water we drink, and our wood comes at a price (5:4). Our fathers sinned and are no more, but we bear their iniquities. 7 Because of This our heart is faint; because of these things our eyes grow dim (5:17). Turn us back to You, O Lord, and we will be "Restored"; Renew our days as of old. 21

Vindicate me, O God, and plead "My Cause" against an ungodly nation; oh, deliver me from the deceitful and unjust man! (Ps. 43:1). Oh, send out Your Light and Your Truth! Let them lead me; let them bring me to Your Holy Hill and to Your Tabernacle. 3 We have heard with our ears, O God, our fathers have told us, the deeds you did in their days, in days of old (Ps. 44:1). You are my King, O God; command victories for Jacob. 4 For I will not trust in my bow, nor shall my sword save me. 6 But you have saved us from our enemies, and have put to shame those who hated us. 7 "In God" we boast all day long, and praise "Your Name" forever. Selah 8 For our soul is bowed down to the dust; our body clings to the ground. 25 Arise for our help, and "Redeem Us for Your Mercies Sake." 26 I will make "Your Name" to be remembered in all generations; therefore the people shall praise You forever and ever (Ps. 45:17).

Great is The Lord, and greatly to be praised in The City of our God, in His Holy Mountain (Ps. 48:1). Beautiful in elevation, The Joy of The Whole Earth, is Mount Zion on the sides of the north, "The City of The Great King." 2 God is in her palaces; He is known as her refuge. 3 For behold, the kings assembled, they passed by together. 4 They saw it, and so they marveled; they were troubled, they hastened away. 5 As we have heard, so we have seemed in The City of The Lord of Hosts, in The City of our God; God will establish it forever. Selah 8 According to "Your Name," O God, so is Your praise to the ends of the earth, Your Right Hand is full of righteousness. 10

But Jesus called them to Himself and said to them, "You know that those who are considered rulers over the Gentiles 'lord it over them,' and their great ones 'exercise authority over them'" (Mark 10:42). "Yet it shall not be so among you; but whoever desires to become great among you shall be your servant." 43 "And whoever of you desires to be first shall be slave of all." 44 "For The Son of Man did not come to be served, but to serve, and to give 'His Life' A Ransom for many." 45

Then He taught, saying to them, "Is it not written, 'My house shall be called A House of Prayer for all nations'? But you have made it 'a den of thieves'" (Mark 11:17). And the scribes and the chief priests heard it and sought how they might destroy Him; for they feared Him, because all the people were astonished at 'His Teaching.' 18 Jesus answered and said to them, "Are you not therefore mistaken, because you do not no 'The Scriptures' nor The Power of God?" (12:24). "So when you see 'The Abomination of Desolation,' spoken of by Daniel the prophet, standing where it ought not" (Let the reader understand), "then let those who are in Judea flee to the mountains."

"For in 'Those Days' there will be tribulation, such as has not been since the beginning of The Creation which God Created until 'This Time,' nor ever shall be" (Mark 13:19). "And unless The Lord had shortened 'Those Days,' 'no flesh' would be saved; but for The Elect's Sake, whom He Chose, 'He Shortened The Days,' 20 "But take heed; See, I have told you all things beforehand." 23

And The Lord said to Moses; "Behold, you will rest with your fathers; and this people will rise and play the harlot with the gods of the foreigners of the land, where they go to be among them, and they will forsake Me and break My Covenant which I made with them" (Deut. 31:16). "Then 'My Anger' shall be aroused against them, and I will forsake them, and I will hide My Face from them, and they shall be devoured. And many evils and troubles shall befall them, so that they say in 'That Day,' 'Have not these evils come upon us because our God is not among us?' 17 "And I will surely hide My Face in 'That Day' because of all the evil which they have done, in that 'they have turned' to other gods." 18 "Then it shall be, when many evils and troubles have come upon them, that this song will testify against them as a witness; for it will not be forgotten in the mouths of their descendants, for 'I Know' the inclination of their behavior today, even before I have brought then to 'The Land' of which I swore to give them." 21

Psalm 74

O God, why have You cast us off forever? Why does Your Anger smoke against The Sheep of Your Pasture? 1 Remember "Your Congregation," which you have purchased of old, The Tribe of Your Inheritance, which "You Have Redeemed"—"This Mount Zion" where You have dwelt. 2 Lift up Your feet to "The Perpetual Desolations." The enemy has damaged everything in the sanctuary. 3 Your enemies roar in the midst of Your meeting place; they set up their banners for signs. 4 They seem like men who lift up axes among the thick trees. 5 And now they break down its carved work, all at once, with axes and hammers. 6 They have set fire to Your Sanctuary; they have defiled The Dwelling Place of Your Name to the ground. 7 They have said in their hearts, "Let us destroy them altogether." They have burned up all The Meeting Places of God in the land. 8 We do not see our signs; there is no longer any prophet; nor is there any among us who knows how long. 9

O God, how long will the adversary reproach? Will the enemy blaspheme Your Name forever? 10 Why do You withdraw You Hand, even Your Right Hand? Take it out of Your bosom and destroy them. 11 For God is my King of old, "Working Salvation" in the midst of the earth. 12 You divided the sea by Your Strength; You broke the heads of the sea serpents in the waters. 13 You broke the heads of Leviathan in pieces, and gave him as food for the people inhabiting the wilderness. 14 You broke open the fountain and the flood; You dried up mighty rivers. 15 The Day is Yours, the night also is Yours; You have prepared "The Light" and the sun. 16 You have set all the borders of the earth; You have made summer and winter. 17

Remember "This," that the enemy has reproached, O Lord, and that a foolish people has blasphemed Your Name. 18 Oh, do not deliver the life of Your turtledove to the wild beast! Do not forget the life of Your poor forever. 19 Have respect to The Covenant; for the dark places of the earth are full of the haunts of cruelty. 20 Oh, do not let the oppressed return ashamed! Let the poor and needy praise Your Name. 21 Arise, O God, "plead Your Own Cause"; remember how the foolish man reproaches You daily. 22 Do not forget the voice of Your enemies; the tumult of those who rise up against You increase continually. 23

And The Word of The Lord came to me, saying (Ezek. 12:21). "Son of man, what is this proverb that you people have about The Land of Israel, which say, 'The Days are prolonged, and every vision fails'? 22 "Tell them therefore, 'Thus says The Lord: "I will lay this proverb to rest, and they shall no more use it as a proverb in Israel."' But say to them, '"The Days are At Hand, and the fulfillment of 'Every Vision.'"

23 "For no more shall there be any false vision or flattering divination within The House of Israel. 24

Now, brethren, concerning The Coming of our Lord Jesus Christ and our "Gathering Together" to Him, we ask you (2 Thess. 2:1). Not to be soon shaken in mind or troubled, either by spirit or by Word or by letter, as if from us, as though The Day of Christ had come. 2 But we are bound to give thanks to God always for you, brethren beloved of The Lord, because God from the beginning "Chose You" for salvation through sanctification by The Spirit and belief in The Truth. 13 To which "He Called You" by our gospel, for The Obtaining of The Glory of Our Lord Jesus Christ. 14

Behold what "Manner of Love" The Father has bestowed upon us, that we should "Be Called" Children of God! Therefore the world does not know us, because it did not know Him (1 John 3:1). Do not marvel, my brethren, if the world hates you. 13 We know that we have passed from death to "Life" because we love "The Brethren." He who does not love his brother abides in death. 14 And every spirit that does not confess that Jesus Christ "Has Come in the flesh is not of God." And this is the spirit of the antichrist, which you have heard was coming, and is now already in the world 4:3 We know that we are of God, and the whole world lies under the sway of the wicked one. 5:19 And we know that The Son of God has come and has given us an understanding, that we may know Him who is True, in His Son Jesus Christ. This is The True God and Eternal Life. 20

For many deceivers have gone out into the world, who do not confess Jesus Christ as coming in the flesh. This is a deceiver and an Antichrist (2 John 1:7). Yet Michael the Archangel, in contending with the devil, when he disputed about the body of Moses, dared not bring against him a reviling accusation, but said, "The Lord rebuke you!" (Jude 1:9). These are spots in your love feasts, while they feast with you without fear, serving only themselves. They are clouds without water, carried away by the winds; late autumn trees without fruit, twice dead, pulled up by the roots; 12 Raging waves of the sea, foaming up their own shame; wandering stars for whom is reserved the blackness of darkness forever. 13

"Take heed to yourselves, lest your heart be deceived, and you turn aside and serve other gods and worship them" (Deut. 11:16). "Therefore you shall lay up 'These Words' of Mine in your heart and in your soul, and bind them as a sign on your hand, and they shall be as frontlets between your eyes." 18 "You shall teach them to your children, speaking of them when you sit in your house, when you walk by 'The Way,' when you lie down, and when you rise up." 19 "And you will write them on your doorposts of your house and on your gates," 20 "That your days and the days of your children may be multiplied in The Land of which The Lord swore to your fathers to give them, like the days of the heavens above the earth." 21 "Every place on which the sole of your feet treads shall be yours: from the wilderness and Lebanon, from the river, the River Euphrates, even to the Western Sea, shall be your territory." 24

The King shall have joy in Your Strength, O Lord; and in Your Salvation how greatly shall He rejoice! (Ps. 21:1). You have given Him His heart's desire, and have not withheld The Request of His Lips. Selah 2 For you meet Him with "The Blessing of Goodness"; You set a crown of pure gold upon His head. 3 He ask "Life" from You, and You give it to Him—length of days forever and ever. 4 His glory is great in Your Salvation; honor and majesty You have placed upon Him. 5 For you have made him most blessed forever; You have made Him exceedingly glad with Your Presence. 6

For The King trusts in The Lord, and through The Mercy of The Most High He shall not be moved. 7 Your Hand will find all Your enemies; Your Right hand will find those who hate You. 8 You will make them as a fiery oven in The Time of Your Anger; The Lord shall swallow them up in His Wrath, and the fire shall devour them. 9 Their offspring You shall destroy from the earth, and their descendants from among The Sons of Men. 10 For they intended evil against You; they devised a plot which they are not able to perform. 11 Therefore You will make them turn their back; You will make ready Your Arrows on Your string toward their faces. 12 Be exalted, O Lord, in Your Own Strength! We will sing and praise Your Power. 13

Does not wisdom cry out, and understanding lift up her voice? (Prov. 8:1). "To you, O men, I Call, and My Voice is to The Sons of Men." 4 The Fear of The Lord is to hate evil; pride and arrogance and the evil way and the perverse mouth I hate. 13 By Me kings reign, and rulers decree justice. 15 "Now therefore, listen to Me, My Children, for blessed are those who keep My Ways." 31 For whoever finds Me finds Life, and obtains favor from The Lord. 35

"Come, eat of My Bread and drink of the wine I have mixed" (Prov. 9:5). Forsake foolishness and Live, and go in "The Way" of understanding. 6 For by Me your days will be multiplied, and years of Life will be added to you. 11 The Fear of The Lord prolongs days, but the years of the wicked will be shortened. 27 The righteous will never be removed, but the wicked will not inhabit the earth.

"Come down and sit in the dust, O Virgin Daughter of Babylon; sit on the ground without a throne, O Daughter of The Chaldeans! For you shall no more be called tender and delicate" (Isa. 47:1). Take the millstones and grind meal. Remove "The Veil," take off the skirt, uncover the thigh, pass through the rivers. 2 Your nakedness shall be uncovered, yes, your shame will be seen; I will take vengeance, and I will not arbitrate with a man." 3 "Sit in silence, and go into darkness, O Daughter of The Chaldeans; for you shall no longer be called The Lady of Kingdoms. 5 I was angry with My People; I have profaned My Inheritance, and given them into your hands. You showed them no mercy; on the elderly you laid your yoke very heavily. 6 And you said, 'I shall be a lady forever,' so that you did not take these things to heart, nor remember The Latter End of them." 7

"Stand now with your enchantments and the multitude of your sorceries, in which you have labored from your youth—perhaps you will be able to profit, perhaps you will prevail. 12 You are wearied in the multitude of your counsels; let now the astrologers, the stargazers, and the monthly prognosticators stand up and save you from what shall come upon you." 13 "You have heard; see all This. And will you declare it? I have made you hear New Things from 'This Time,' even hidden things, and you did not know them" (48:6). "Surely you did not hear, surely you did not know; surely from long ago your ear was not opened. For I knew that you would deal very treacherously, and were called a transgressor from the womb." 8

"Listen to Me, O Jacob, and Israel, My Called: I Am He, I Am 'The First,' I Am also 'The Last.'" 12 "All of you, assemble yourselves, and hear! Who among them has declared 'These Things'? The Lord Loves Him; He shall do his pleasure on Babylon, and His Arm shall be against the Chaldeans." 14 "Come near to Me, hear This: I have not spoken in secret from the beginning; from the time that it was, I Was There. And 'NOW' The Lord God and His Spirit have sent Me." 16 Oh, that you had heeded "My Commandments"! Then your peace would have been like a river, and your righteousness like the waves of the sea. 18

Why, when I came, was there no man? Why, when I called, was there none to answer? Is My Hand shortened at all that it cannot "Redeem"? Or have I no power to "Deliver"? Indeed with "My Rebuke" I dry up the sea, I make the rivers a wilderness; their fish stink because there is no water, and die of thirst (50:2). The Lord God has given Me The Tongue of The Learned, that I should know how to speak "A Word" in season to him that is weary. He awakens Me morning by morning, He awakens My Ear to hear as The Learned. 4

For The Lord will comfort Zion, He will comfort all her waste places; He will make her wilderness like Eden, and her desert; like "The Garden of The Lord"; joy and gladness will be found in it, thanksgiving and the voice of melody (51:3). Awake, awake, put on strength, O Arm of The Lord! Awake as in The Ancient Days, in The Generations of Old. Are you not "The Arm" that cut Rahab apart, and wounded the serpent? 9 Are you not "The One" who dried up the sea, the waters of the great deep; that made the depths of the sea a road for "The Redeemed" to cross over? 10

The Lord has made bare "His Holy Arm" in The Eyes of All The Nations, All the ends of the earth shall see "The Salvation of Our God" (52:10). So shall He sprinkle many nations. Kings shall shut their mouths at Him; for what had not been told them they shall see, and what they had not heard they shall consider. 15 Whom do you ridicule? Against whom do you make a wide mouth and stick out the tongue? Are you not children of transgression, offspring of falsehood (57:4). Inflaming yourselves with gods under every green tree, slaying the children in the valleys, under the clefts of the rocks? 5 I will declare your righteousness and your works, for they will not profit you. 12 When you cry out, let your collection of idols deliver you. But the wind will carry them all away. a breath will take them, but he who puts his trust in Me shall possess the land, and shall inherit "My Holy Mountain." 13

For thus says "The High and Lofty Ones" who inhabits Eternity, whose name is Holy: "I will dwell in 'The High and Holy Place, with him who has a contrite and humble spirit, to 'Revive' the spirit of the humble, and to 'Revive' the heart of the contrite ones. 15 Then you shall call, and The Lord will answer; you shall cry, and He will say, 'Here I am.' If you take away the yoke from your midst, the pointing of the finger, and speaking wickedness" (58:9).

The Lord has done what He purposed; He has fulfilled His Word which He has commanded in days of old. He has thrown down and has not pitied, and He has caused an enemy to rejoice over you; He has exalted the hand of your adversaries (Lam. 2:17). Their heart cried out to The Lord, "O Wall of The Daughter of Zion, let tears run down like a river day and night; give yourself no relief; give your eyes no rest. 18 Arise, cry out in the night, at The Beginning of The Watches; pour out your heart like water before The Face of The Lord. Lift your hands towards Him for The Life of your young children, who faint from hunger at the head of every street." 19

My eyes bring suffering to My Soul because of all the daughters of my city (3:51). My enemies without cause hunted me down like a bird. 52 They silenced My Life in the pit and threw stones at Me. 53 The waters flowed over My head; I said, "I am cut off!" 54 O Lord, You have seen how I am wronged; Judge My Case. 59 You have seen all their vengeance, all their schemes against Me. 60 You have heard their reproach, all their schemes against Me. 61 Repay them, O Lord, according to the works of their hands. 64 Give them a vile heart; Your

Curse be upon them! 65 In Your Anger, pursue and destroy them from under The Heavens of The Lord. 66

"For with what judgment you judge, you will be judged; and with the measure you use, it will be measured back to you" (Matt. 7:2). "Ask, and it will be given to you; seek, and you will find; knock, and it will be opened to you." 7 "For everyone who asks receives, and he who seeks finds, and to him who knocks it will be opened." 8 "Therefore, whatever you want men to do for you, do also to them, for This is The Law and The Prophets." 12 "Because narrow is The Gate and difficult is 'The Way' which leads to Life, and there are few who find it." 14 "Therefore whoever hears these sayings of Mine, and does them, I will liken him to a wise man who built his house on 'The Rock.'" 24

"Declare among the nations, proclaim, and set up a standard; proclaim—do not conceal it—say, 'Babylon is taken, Bel is shamed; Marduk is broken in pieces; her idols are humiliated, her images are broken in pieces'" (Jer. 50:2). "Because you were glad, because you rejoiced, you destroyers of My Heritage, because you have grown fat like a heifer threshing grain, and you bellow like bulls, 11 Your mother shall be deeply ashamed; she who bore you shall be ashamed, Behold, the least of the nations shall be a wilderness, a dry land and a desert." 12

Yet for Us there is "One God," "The Father," of whom are all things, and We for Him; and "One Lord Jesus Christ," through whom are all things, and through whom We Live (1 Cor. 8:6). Am I not an apostle? Am I not free? Have I not seen Jesus Christ our Lord? Are you not "My Work" in The Lord? (9:1). For if I preach "The Gospel," I have nothing to boast of, for necessity is laid upon me; yes, woe is me if I do not preach "The Gospel"! 16 What is my reward then? That when I preach "The Gospel," I may present "The Gospel of Christ" without charge, that I may not abuse "My Authority" in "The Gospel." 18 Now "This" I do for "The Gospel's Sake," that I may be partaker of it with you. 23

Moreover, brethren, I do not want you to be unaware that all our fathers were under the cloud, all passed through the sea (10:1). All were baptized into Moses in the cloud and in the sea, 2 All ate the same "Spiritual Food," 3 And all drank the same "Spiritual Drink." For they drank of that "Spiritual Rock" that followed them, and "That Rock" was "Christ." 4 You cannot drink "The Cup of The Lord" and the cup of demons; you cannot partake of "The Lord's Table" and of the table of demons. 21 Or do we provoke The Lord to jealousy? Are we stronger "Then He"? 22

God came from Teman, "The Holy One" from Mount Paran. Selah. His Glory covered the heavens, and the earth was full of His Praise (Hab. 3:3). His brightness was like "The Light"; He had rays flashing from His Hand, and there His Power was hidden. 4 Before Him went pestilence, and "Fever" followed at His Feet. 5 He stood and measured the earth; He looked and startled the nations. And "The Everlasting Mountains" were scattered, The Perpetual Hills bowed. "His Ways" are "Everlasting."

Your Bow was made quite ready; Oaths were sworn over Your Arrows. Selah. You divided the earth with rivers. 9 The Mountains saw You and trembled; the overflowing of the waters passed by. The deep uttered its voice, and lifted its hands on high. 10 The sun and the moon stood still in their habitation; at "The Light" of Your Arrows they went, at The Shining of Your Glittering Spear. 11 You marched through the land in Indignation; you trampled the nations in Anger. 12 You went forth for "The Salvation of Your People," for Salvation with Your Anointed.

You struck the head from the house of the wicked, by laying bare from foundation to neck. Selah. 13

Gather yourselves together, yes, gather together, O undesirable nation (Zeph. 2:1). Before "The Decree" is issued, or the day passes like chaff, before The Lord's Fierce Anger comes upon you, before The Day of The Lord's Anger comes upon you! 2 "Therefore wait for Me," says The Lord, "Until The Day I rise up for plunder; My Determination is to 'Gather The Nations' to 'My Assembly of Kingdoms,' to pour on them My Indignation, all My Fierce Anger; all the earth shall be devoured with 'The Fire of My Jealousy'" (3:8). "For then I Will Restore to the people 'A Pure Language,' that they all may 'Call on The Name of The Lord,' to 'Serve Him With One Accord.'" 9

"Do not be like your fathers, to whom the former prophets preached, saying, 'Thus says The Lord of Hosts: Turn Now from you evil ways and your evil deeds.'" "But they did not hear nor heed Me," says The Lord (Zech. 1:4). Yet surely My Words and My Statutes, which I commanded My servants the prophets, did they not overtake your fathers? "So they 'Returned' and said: 'Just as The Lord of Hosts determined to do to us, according to our ways and according to our deeds, so He has dealt with us.'" 6

"Sing and Rejoice, O Daughter of Zion! For behold, I AM Coming and I will dwell in your midst," says The Lord (2:10). "Many nations shall be joined to The Lord in that day, and they shall become 'My People.' And I will dwell in your midst. Then you will know that The Lord of Hosts has 'Sent Me' to you." 11 "And The Lord will take Possession of Judah as His Inheritance in The Holy Land, and will again choose Jerusalem." 12 "Be silent, all flesh, before The Lord, for He is aroused from His Holy Habitation!" 13

"Then I pleaded with The Lord at that time saying" (Deut. 3:23). "O Lord God, You have begun to show Your Servant Your Greatness and Your Mighty Hand, for what god is there in heaven or on earth who can do anything like Your Works and Your Mighty Deeds?" 24 "I pray, let me cross over and see 'The Good Land' beyond the Jordan, those Pleasant Mountains and Lebanon." 25 "So we stayed in the valley opposite Beth-Peor." 29

"Now, O Israel, listen to The Statutes and The Judgments which I teach you to observe, that you may Live, and go in and possess 'The Land' which The Lord God of your fathers is giving you" (4:1). "You shall not add to 'The Word' which I command you, nor take from It, that you may keep The Commandments of The Lord your God which I command you." 2 "Your eyes have seen what The Lord did at Baal Peor; for The Lord your God has destroyed from among you all the men who followed Baal of Peor." 3 "But you who held fast to The Lord your God are Alive today, every one of you." 4

And Moses called all Israel, and said to them: "Hear, O Israel, The Statutes and Judgments which I speak in you hearing today, that you may learn them and be careful to observe them" (5:1). "The Lord did not make This Covenant with our fathers, but with us, those who are here Today, all of us who are Alive." 3 "I stood between The Lord and you at 'That Time, to 'Declare to You' The Word of The Lord; for you were afraid because of the fire, and you did not go up The Mountain. He Said: 5 'I Am The Lord you God who brought you out of the land of Egypt, out of the house of bondage. 6 You shall have no other gods before Me.'" 7 "Oh, that they had such a heart in them that they would Fear Me and always keep My Commandments, that it might be well with them and with their children forever!" 29

"When your son ask you in time to come, saying, 'What is The Meaning of The Testimonies, The Statutes. and The Judgments which The Lord our God commanded you?'" (6:20). "Then you shall say to your son: 'We were slaves of Pharaoh in Egypt, and The Lord brought us out of Egypt with A Mighty Hand; 21 and The Lord showed "signs and wonders" before our eyes, "great and severe," against Egypt, Pharaoh, and all his household. 22 Then He brought us out from there, that He might bring us in, to give us the land of which He swore to our fathers. 23 And The Lord commanded us to observe all these statutes, to fear The Lord our God, "for our good always," that He might preserve us "Alive," as it is "This Day." 24 Then it will be "Righteousness For Us," if we are careful to observe all these commandments before The Lord our God, as He has commanded us.'" 25

"For you are 'A Holy People' to The Lord your God; The Lord your God has 'Chosen You' to be 'A People' for Himself, 'A Special Treasure' above all the peoples of the earth'" (7:6). The Lord did not set His Love on you nor choose you because were more in number than any other people, for you were the least of all peoples; 7 But because 'The Lord Loves You,' and because He would keep The Oath which He swore to your fathers, The Lord has brought you out with 'A Mighty Hand,' and 'Redeemed You' from the house of bondage, from the hand of Pharaoh king of Egypt. 8 Therefore know the Lord your God, He is God, 'The Faithful God' who keeps 'Covenant and Mercy' for a thousand generations with those who love Him and keep His Commandments; 9 And The Lord will take away from you 'All' sickness, and will afflict you with none of the terrible diseases of Egypt which you have known, but will lay them on all those who hate you." 15

"You should know in your heart that as a man chastens his son, so 'The Lord you God Chastens You'" (8:5). Beware that you do not forget The

Lord your God by not keeping His Commandments, His Judgments, and His Statutes which I command you 'Today,' 11 Then it shall be, if you by any means forget The Lord you God, and follow other gods, and serve them and worship them, I Testify Against you 'This Day' that you shall surely perish." 19

Give ear, O My People, to My Law; incline your ears to The Words of My Mouth (Ps. 78:1). We will not hide them from their children, telling to the generation to come The Praises of The Lord, and His Strength and His Wonderful Works that He has done. 4 For He established 'A Testimony' in Jacob, and appointed 'A Law' in Israel, which He commanded our fathers, that they should make them known to their children; 5 That 'The Generation to Come' might know them, the children who would be born, that they may Arise and Declare them to their children, 6 That they may 'Set Their Hope' in God, and not forget The Works of God, but keep His Commandments; 7 And may not be like their fathers, a stubborn and rebellious generation, a generation that did not 'Set Its Heart Aright,' and whose spirit was not faithful to God. 8 Nevertheless they flattered Him with their mouth, and they lied unto Him with their tongue; 36 For their heart was not steadfast with Him, nor where they faithful in His Covenant. 37 Yes, again and again they tempted God, and limited The Holy One of Israel. 41 They did not remember His Power: The Day when He Redeemed them from the enemy, 42

Do not keep silent, O God! Do not hold Your peace, and do not be still, O God! (Ps. 83:1). For Behold, Your enemies make a tumult; and those who hate You have lifted up their head. 2 They have taken crafty counsel against Your People, and consulted together against Your sheltered ones. 3 They have said, "Come, and let us cut them off from being a nation, that The Name of Israel may be remembered no more." 4 For they have consulted together with one consent; they form a confederacy against You: 5

O My God, make them like the whirling dust, like the chaff before the wind! 13 As the fire burns the woods, and as the flame sets the mountains on fire, 14 So pursue them with Your tempest, and frighten them with Your storm. 15 Fill their face with shame, that they may seek Your Name, O Lord. 16 Let them be confounded and dismayed forever; yes, let them be put to shame and perish. 17 That they may know that You, whose name alone is The Lord, are The Most High over all the earth.

Tsade

Righteous are You, O Lord, and Upright are Your Judgments (Ps. 119:137). Your Testimonies, which You have commanded, are righteous and very faithful. 138 My zeal has consumed me, because me enemies have forgotten Your Words. 139 Your Word is very pure; therefore Your Servants love it. 140 I am small and despised, yet I do not forget Your Precepts. 141

Your Righteousness is an Everlasting Righteousness, and Your Law is Truth. 142 Trouble and anguish have overtaken me, yet Your Commandments are my delights. 143 The Righteousness of Your Testimonies is everlasting; give me understanding, and I shall Live. 144

And He said to Me, "Son of man, stand on your feet, and I will speak to You" (Ezek. 2:1). "Then 'The Spirit' entered Me when He Spoke to Me, and set Me on My Feet: and I Heard Him who Spoke To Me. 2 And He said to Me, "Son of man, I am sending You to 'The Children,' to A Rebellious Nation who has rebelled against Me; they and their fathers have transgressed against Me to 'This Very Day.'" 3 "You shall speak My Words to them, whether they hear or whether they refuse, for they are rebellious." 7 "But you, Son of man, hear what I say to You. Do not be rebellious like that rebellious house; open Your mouth and eat what I give You." 8 Moreover He said to Me: "Son of man, receive into Your heart all My Words that I speak to You, and hear with Your ears." 10

Now "The End" has come upon you, and I will send My anger against you; I will judge you according to your ways, and I will repay you for all your abominations (7:3). "My eye will not spare, nor will I have pity; I will repay you according to your ways, and your abominations will be in your midst." Then you shall know that I Am The Lord who strikes. 9 The Sword is outside, and the pestilence and famine within. Whosoever is in the field will die by The Sword; and whoever is in the city, famine and pestilence will devour him. 15 Those who survive will escape and be on the mountains like dove of the valleys, all of them mourning, each for his iniquity. 16 Then He said to Me, "The iniquity of The House of Israel and Judah is exceedingly great, and the land is full of bloodshed, and the city full of perversity; for they say, 'The Lord has forsaken the land, and The Lord does not see!'" (Ezek. 9:9).

The fool has said in his heart, "There is no God." They are corrupt, and have done abominable iniquity; there is none who does good (Ps. 53:1). God looks down from heaven upon "The Children of men," to see if there are any who understand, who Seek God. 2 There they are in great fear where "no fear" was, for God has scattered the bones of him who encamps against you, you have put them to shame, because God has despised them. 5 Oh, that "The Salvation" of Israel would come out of Zion! When God brings back The Captivity of His People, let Jacob rejoice and Israel be glad. 6

And He said: "The Lord roars from Zion, and utter His Voice from Jerusalem; the pastures of the shepherds mourn, and the top of Carmel withers" (Amos 1:2). I Raised up some of your sons as prophets, and some of your young men as "Nazirites." Is it not so, O Children of Israel? (2:11). "But you gave the 'Nazirites' wine to drink, and commanded the prophets saying, 'Do Not Prophesy!'" 12

"Therefore flight shall perish from the swift, the strong shall not strengthen his power, no shall the mighty deliver himself; 14 He shall not stand who handles the bow, the swift of foot shall not escape, nor shall he who rides a horse deliver himself. 15 The most courageous men of might shall flee naked in 'That Day,'" says The Lord.

If "A Trumpet" is blown in a city, will not the people be afraid? If there is calamity in a city, will not The Lord have done it? (3:6). Surely The Lord God does nothing, unless "He Reveals" His Secret to His Servants the prophets. 7 A lion roared! Who will not fear? The Lord God Has Spoken! Who can but prophesy? 8

For they do not know to do right, says The Lord, "Who store up violence and robbery in their palaces." 10 Therefore thus says The Lord God: "An adversary shall be all around the land; he shall sap your strength from you, and your palaces shall be plundered." 11 The Lord God has sworn by His Holiness: "Behold, The Day shall come upon you when He will take you away with fishhooks, and your posterity with fishhooks" (4:2).

"Seek The Lord and 'Live,' lest He break out like fire in The House of Joseph, and devour it, with no one to quench it in Bethel" (5:6). You who turn justice to wormwood, and lay righteousness to rest in the earth!" 7 He made the Pleiades and Orion: He turns The Shadow of

Death into morning and makes the day dark as the night; He calls for the waters of the sea and pours them out on The Face of The Earth; The Lord is His Name. 8

He rains ruin upon the strong, so that fury comes upon the fortress. 9 They hate "The One" who rebukes in the gate, and they abhor "The One" who speaks Uprightly. 10 Therefore, because you tread down the poor and take grain taxes from him, though you have built houses of hewn stone, you shall not dwell in them; you have planted pleasant vineyards, but you shall not drink from them. 11 For I know your manifold transgressions and your mighty sins: afflicting The Just and taking bribes; diverting the poor from justice at the gate. 12 Therefore the prudent keep silent at that time, for it is "An Evil Time." 13 Is not The Day of The Lord darkness, and not light? Is it not very dark, with no brightness in it? 20

Who can stand before His Indignation? And who can endure The Fierceness of His Anger? His Fury is poured out like fire, and the rocks are thrown down by Him (Nahum 1:6). The Lord is Good, A Stronghold in The Day of Trouble; and He Knows those who trust in Him. 7 When I heard, my body trembled; my lips quivered at "The Voice"; rottenness entered my bones; and I trembled in myself, that I might rest in The Day of Trouble. When He comes up to the people, He will invade them with His troops (Hab. 3:16). Though the fig tree may not blossom, nor fruit be on the vines; though the labor of the olive may fail, and the fields yield no fruit; though the flock may be cut off from the fold, and there be no herd in the stalls. 17

"I will utterly consume everything from The Face of The Earth," says The Lord (Zeph. 1:2). "I will consume man and beast; I will consume the birds of the heavens, the fish of the sea, and the stumbling blocks with the wicked. I will cut off man from The Face of The Earth," says The Lord. 3 "I will stretch out My Hand against Judah, and against of The Inhabitants of Jerusalem. I will cut off every trace of Baal from this place, the names of the idolatrous priests with the pagan priests." 4

Seek The Lord, all you meek of the earth, who have upheld His Justice. Seek Righteousness, seek humility. It may be that you will be hidden in The Day of The Lord's Anger (2:3). Woe to her who is rebellious and polluted, to the oppressing city! (3:1). She has not obeyed His Voice, she has not received correction; she has not trusted in The Lord, she has not drawn near to her God. 2 So Israel was joined to Baal of Peor, and The Anger of The Lord was aroused against Israel (Num. 25:3).

"This is The Word which The Lord has spoken concerning him: 'The virgin, The Daughter of Zion, has despised you, laughed you to scorn; The Daughter of Jerusalem has shaken her head behind your back!'" (Isa. 37:22). "Whom have you reproached and blasphemed? Against whom have raised your voice, and lifted up your eyes on high? Against The Holy One of Israel." 23 "I have dug and drunk water, and with the soles of my feet I have dried up all the brooks of defense." 25 "Did you not hear long ago how I made it, from ancient times that I formed it? Now I have brought it to pass, that you should be for crushing fortified cities into heaps of ruins. 26 Therefore their inhabitants had little power; they were dismayed and confounded; they were as grass of the field and the green herb, as the grass on the housetops and grain blighted before it is grown. 27

"Behold, The Days are Coming when all that is in your house, and what your fathers have accumulated until 'This Day,' shall be carried to Babylon; nothing shall be left,' says The Lord" (39:6). "Comfort, yes, comfort My People!" says your God (40:1). "Speak comfort to Jerusalem, and cry out to her, that her warfare has ended, that her iniquity is pardoned; for she has received form The Lord's Hand double for all her sins." 2 The Glory of The Lord shall be revealed, and All Flesh shall see it together; for The Mouth of The Lord has spoken." 5 The Voice said, "Cry out!" and He said, "What shall I cry?' "All flesh is grass, and all its loveliness is like the flower of the field. 6 The grass withers, the flower fades, because The Breath of The Lord blows upon it; surely the people are the grass. 7 The grass withers, the flower fades, but The Word of The Lord stands forever." 8

Behold, The Lord God shall come with "A Strong Hand," and His Arm shall rule for Him; behold. His Reward is with Him, and His work before Him. 10 He will feed His Flock like a shepherd; He will gather the lambs with His Arm, and carry them in His bosom, and "Gently Lead" those who are with young. 11 He brings the princes to nothing; He makes the judges of the earth useless. 23 Scarcely shall they be planted, scarcely shall they be sown, scarcely shall their stock take root in the earth, when He will blow on them, and they will wither, and the whirlwind will take them away like stubble. 24

Why do you say, O Jacob, and speak, O Israel: "My way is hidden from The Lord, and my just claim is passed over by My God"? 27 Have you not known? Have you not heard? The Everlasting God, The Lord, The Creator of The Ends of The Earth, neither faints nor is weary. His Understanding is unsearchable. 28 He Gives power to the weak, and to those who have no might He Increases Strength. 29

"But you, Israel, are My servant, Jacob whom I have Chosen, The Descendants of Abraham 'My Friend'" (41:8). You whom I have taken from The Ends of The Earth, and Called from its farthest regions, and said to you, "You are My Servant, I have Chosen You and have not cast you away: 9 Fear not, for I am with you; be not dismayed, for I Am your God. I will strengthen you, yes, I will help you, I will uphold you with 'My Righteous Right Hand.'" 10

"Behold! My Servant whom I uphold, 'My Elect One' in whom My Soul delights! I have put 'My Spirit' upon Him; He will bring forth justice to the Gentiles" (42:1). "He will not fail nor be discouraged, till He has established justice in the earth; and the coastlands shall wait for His Law." 4 "I, The Lord, have called you in righteousness, and will hold Your Hand; I will keep You and give You as 'A Covenant' to the people, as 'A Light' to the Gentiles. 6 To open blind eyes, to bring out prisoners from the prison, those who sit in darkness from the prison house. 7 I will bring the blind by a way they did not know; I will lead them in paths they have not known, I will make darkness light before them, and crooked places straight. These things I will do for them, and not forsake them." 16

But now, thus says The Lord, who created you, O Jacob, and He who formed you, O Israel: "Fear not, for I have redeemed you; I have called you by your name; you are Mine (43:1). And who can proclaim as I do? Then let him declare it and set it in order for me, since I appointed the ancient people. And the things that are coming and shall come, let them show these to them (44:7). Those who make an image, all of them are useless, and their precious things shall not profit; they are their own witnesses; they neither see nor know, that they may be ashamed. 9 "And you have lifted yourself up against The Lord of heaven. They have brought the vessels of His House before you, and you and your lords, your wives and your concubines, have drunk wine from them. And you have praised the god of silver and gold, bronze and iron, wood and stone, which do not see or hear or know; and The God who holds your breath in His Hand and owns all your ways, "You Have Not Glorified" (Dan. 5:23).

Give unto The Lord, O you mighty ones, give unto The Lord glory and strength (Ps. 29:1). Give unto The Lord The Glory due to His Name; worship The Lord in The Beauty of Holiness. 2 I will extol You, O Lord, for you have lifted me up, you have not let my foes rejoice over me (30:1). O Lord My God, I cried out to You, and you healed Me. 2 O Lord, You brought My soul up from the grave; You have Kept Me Alive, that I should not go to The Pit. 3 Sing praise to The Lord, you saints of His, and give thanks at The Remembrance of His Holy Name. 4

Oh, clap your hands, all you peoples! Shout to God with The Voice of Triumph! (Ps. 47:1). For The Lord Most High is awesome; He is A Great King over all the earth. 2 He will subdue the peoples under us, and the nations under our feet. 3 He will choose our inheritance for us, The Excellence of Jacob whom He Loves. Selah 4 God has gone up with a shout, The Lord with The Sound of A Trumpet. 5 Sing praises to God, sing praises! Sing praises to Our King, sing praises! 6 For God is The King of All The Earth; sing praises with understanding. 7 God reigns over the nations; God sit on His Holy Throne. 8 The princes of the people have gathered together, The People of The God of Abraham. For The Shields of the earth belong to God; He is Greatly Exalted. 9

Now The Lord had said to Abram: "Get out of your country, from your family and from your father's house, to a land that I will show you" (Gen. 12:1). "I will make you a great nation; I will bless you and make your name great; and you shall be a blessing. 2 I will bless those who bless you, and I will curse him who curses you; and in you all the families of the earth shall be blessed." 3

The heavens declare The Glory of God; and the firmament shows His Handiwork (Ps. 19:1). Day unto day utters speech, and night unto night reveals knowledge. 2 There is no speech nor language where their voice is not heard. 3 Their line has gone out through all the earth, and Their Words to the end of the world. In "Them" He has set A Tabernacle for the sun, 4 Which is like A Bridegroom coming out of his chamber, and rejoices like a strong man to run its race. 5 Its Rising is from one end of heaven, and its circuit to the other end; and there is nothing hidden from its heat. 6

The Law of The Lord is "Perfect," converting the soul; The Testimony of The Lord is "Sure," making wise the simple. 7 The Statutes of The Lord are "Right," rejoicing the heart; The Commandment of The Lord is "Pure," Enlightening the eyes; 8 The Fear of The Lord is "Clean," Enduring Forever; The Judgments of The Lord are "True and Righteous" altogether. 9 More to be desired are "They" than gold, yea, than much fine gold; sweeter also than honey and the honeycomb. 10

Moreover by "Them" Your servant is warned, and in keeping "Them" there is great reward. 11 Who can understand his errors? Cleanse me from secret faults. 12 Keep back Your servant also from presumptuous sins; let them not have dominion over me. Then I shall be blameless, and I shall be innocent of great transgression. 13 Let the words of my mouth and the meditation of my heart be acceptable in Your Sight, O Lord, My Strength and My Redeemer. 14

May The Lord answer you in The Day of Trouble; may The Name of The God of Jacob defend you (Ps. 20:1). May He send you help from The Sanctuary, and strengthen you Out of Zion; 2 May He remember all your offerings, and accept your burnt sacrifice. Selah 3 May He grant you according to your heart's desire, and fulfill all your purpose. 4 We will rejoice in Your Salvation, and in The Name of Our God we will set up Our Banners! May The Lord fulfill all your petitions. 5

Now I Know that The Lord saves His Anointed; He will answer Him from His Holy Heaven with The Saving Strength of His Right Hand. 6 Some trust in chariots, and some in horses; but we will remember The Name of The Lord our God. 7 They have bowed down and fallen; but we have "Risen and Stand Upright." 8 Save Lord! May The King answer us when we call. 9

"Behold, The Days are Coming," says The Lord, "That I will raise to David 'A Branch of Righteousness'; A King shall reign and prosper. and execute judgment and righteousness in the earth" (Jer. 23:5). In "His Days" Judah will be saved, and Israel will dwell safely; now this is His Name by which He will be called; The Lord our Righteousness.

For I know the thoughts that I think toward you, says The Lord, Thoughts of peace and not of evil, to give you a future and a hope (29:11). Then you will call upon Me and go and pray to Me, and I will listen to you. 12 And you will seek Me and find Me, when you search for Me with all your heart. 13 I will be found by you, says The Lord, and I will bring you back from your captivity; I will gather you from all the nations and from all the places where I have driven you, says The Lord, and I will bring you to the place from which I cause you to be carried away captive. 14

Then the secret was revealed to Daniel in A Night Vision. So Daniel Blessed The God of Heaven (Dan. 2:19). Daniel answered and said: "Blessed be The Name of God forever and ever, for wisdom and might are His. 20 And He changes The Times and The Seasons; He removes kings and Raises Up Kings: He Gives Wisdom to The Wise and

Knowledge to those who have Understanding. 21 He Reveals deep and secret things: He Knows what is in darkness, and Light Dwells with Him. 22 'I thank You and praise You, O God of my fathers; you have given me wisdom and might, and have now made known to me what we ask of You, for You have made known to us the king's demand.'" 23

"But there is A God in Heaven who reveals secret, and He has made known to King Nebuchadnezzar what will be 'In The Latter Days.' Your dream, and the visions of your head upon your bed, were these." 28 "And in The Days of these kings The God of Heaven will Set Up A Kingdom which shall never be destroyed; and The Kingdom shall not be left to other people; it shall break in pieces and consume all these kingdoms, and it shall stand forever." 44

I thought it good To Declare The Signs and Wonders that The Most High God has worked for me (Dan. 4:2). How great are His Signs, and How Mighty are His Wonders! His Kingdom is an everlasting Kingdom, and His Dominion is from generation to generation. 3 "This decision is by The Decree of The Watchers, and The Sentence by The Word of The Holy Ones, in order that the living may know that The Most High Rules in The Kingdom of Men, gives it to whoever He Will, and set over it the lowest of men." 17 All the inhabitants of the earth are reputed as nothing; He does according to His Will in The Army of Heaven and among the inhabitants of the earth. No one can restrain His Hand or say to Him, "What have You done?"

In The Beginning God Created The Heavens and The Earth (Gen. 1:1). Then God said, "Let there be Light"; and there was Light. 2 This is The History of The Heavens and The Earth when They Were Created, in The Day that The Lord God made the earth and the heavens (2:4).

Hear My Words, you wise men; give ear to Me, you who have knowledge (Job 34:2). For the ear tests words as the palate tastes food. 3 Let us choose Justice for ourselves; let us know among ourselves what is good. 4 "Therefore listen to me, you men of understanding: far be it from God to do wickedness, and from The Almighty to commit iniquity. 10 For He repays man according to his work, and makes man to find a reward according to His Way. 11 Surely God will never do wickedness, nor will The Almighty pervert justice." 12

"If you have understanding, Hear This; listen to The Sound of My Word: 16 Should one who hates justice govern? Will you condemn Him who is Most Just? 17 Is it fitting to say to a king, 'You are worthless,' and to nobles, 'You are wicked'? 18 Yet He is not partial to princes, nor does He regard the rich man more than the poor; for they all are The Work of His Hands. 19 In a moment they die, in the middle of the night; the people are shaken and pass away; the mighty are taken away without a hand." 20 "For His Eyes are on the ways of man, and He Sees all his steps." 21

"Bear with me a little while, and I will show you that there are yet Words to speak on God's behalf" (36:2). For truly My Words are not false; One who is perfect in knowledge is with you. 4 "Behold, God is Mighty, but despises no one; He is Mighty in Strength of Understanding. 5 He does not preserve the life of the wicked, but give justice to the oppressed. 6 He also opens their ears to instruction, and commands that they turn from iniquity. 10 If they obey and serve Him, they shall spend their days in prosperity, and their years in pleasure. 11 But if they do not obey, they shall perish by The Sword, and they shall die without knowledge. 12 Because there is wrath, beware lest He take you away with one blow; for a large ransom would not help you avoid it." 18

"Behold, God is exalted by His Power; who teaches like Him? 22 Who has assigned Him His Way, or who has said, 'You have done wrong'?" 23 "Remember to Magnify His Work, of which men have sung." 24 Everyone has seen it; man looks on it from afar. 25 Behold, God is great, and we do not Know Him; nor can the number of His years be discovered. 26 For He draws up drops of water, which distill as rain from the mist, 27 Which the clouds drop down and pour abundantly on man. 28 For by these He Judges the peoples; He gives food in abundance. 31 He causes it To Come, whether for correction, or for His Land, or for mercy (37:13).

O Lord, You have searched me and known me (Ps. 139:1). You know my sitting down and my rising up; You understand my thought afar off. 2 You comprehend my path and my lying down, and are acquainted with all my ways. 3 For there is not a word on my tongue, but Behold, O Lord, You know it altogether. 4 I will praise You, for I am fearfully and wonderfully made; marvelous are Your Works, and that my soul knows very well. 14 Search me, O God, and know my heart; try me, and know my anxieties; 23 And see if there is any wicked way in me, and lead me in The Way Everlasting. 24

Preserve me, O God, for in You I put my trust (Ps. 16:1). O my soul, you have said to The Lord, "You are my Lord, my goodness is nothing apart from you." 2 As for the saints who are on the earth, "They are The Excellent Ones, in whom is all me delight." 3 Their sorrows shall be multiplied who hasten after another god; their drink offering of blood I will not offer, nor take up their names on my lips. 4 O Lord, You are my portion of my inheritance and my cup; You maintain my lot. 5

The lines have fallen to me in pleasant places; yes, I will have a good inheritance. 6 I will bless The Lord who has given me counsel; my heart also instructs me in the night seasons. 7 I have set The Lord always before me; because He is at My Right Hand I shall not be moved. 8 Therefore my heart is glad, and my glory rejoices; my flesh also will rest in hope. 9 For You will not leave my soul in Sheol, nor will You allow Your Holy One to see corruption. 10 You will show me The Path of Life; in Your Presence is fullness of joy; at Your Right Hand are pleasures forevermore. 11

For Thus says The Lord: "We have heard a voice of trembling, of fear, and not of peace" (Jer. 30:5). Ask now, and see, whether a man is ever in labor with child? So why do I see every man with his hands on his loins like a woman in labor, and all faces turned pale? 6 Alas! For that day is great, so that none is like it; and it is The Time of Jacob's Trouble, but he shall be saved out of it. 7 "For it shall come to pass in that day," says The Lord of hosts, "That I will break his yoke from your neck, and will burst your bonds; foreigners shall no more enslave them. 8 But they shall serve The Lord their God, and David their King, whom I Will Raise up to them." 9

"'Therefore do not fear, O My servant Jacob,' says The Lord, 'Nor be dismayed, O Israel; for behold, I will save you from afar, and your seed from the land of their captivity. Jacob Shall Return, have rest and be quiet, and no one shall make him afraid, 10 For I Am with you,' says The Lord, to Save You; though I make a full end of all nations where I have scattered you, yet I will not make a complete end of you. But I will correct you In Justice, and will not let you go altogether unpunished.'" 11

"For thus says The Lord: 'Your affliction is incurable, your wound is severe. 12 There is no one to plead your cause, that you may be bound up; you have no healing medicines. 13 All your lovers have forgotten you; they do not seek you; for I have wounded you with the wound of an enemy, with the chastisement of a cruel one, for the multitude of your iniquities, because your sins have increased. 14 Why do you cry about your affliction? Your sorrow is incurable. Because of the multitude of your iniquities, because your sins have increased, I have done these things to you.'" 15

"'Therefore all those who devour you shall be devoured; and all your adversaries, every one of them, shall go into captivity; those who plunder you shall become plunder, and all who prey upon you I will make a prey. 16 For I Will Restore health to you and heal you of your wounds,' says The Lord, 'Because they called you an outcast saying: "This is Zion; no one seeks her."'" 17

O Zion, you who bring good tidings, get up into the high mountains; O Jerusalem, you who bring good tidings, lift up your voice with strength, lift it up, be not afraid; say to the cities of Judah, "Behold Your God!" (Isa. 40:9). Behold, The Lord God shall come with a strong hand, and His Arm shall rule for Him; behold, His Reward is with Him, and His Work before Him. 10 He will feed His Flock like a shepherd; He will gather the lambs with His Arm, and carry them in His bosom, and gently lead those who are with young. 11

For thus says The Lord God: "Indeed I Myself will search for My Sheep and seek them out" (Ezek. 34:11). "As a shepherd seeks out his flock on the day he is among his scattered sheep, so I Will Seek Out My Sheep and Deliver Them from all the places where they were scattered on A Cloudy and Dark Day." 12 "And I Will Bring Them out from the peoples and Gather Them from the countries, and will bring them to Their Own Land; I will feed them on the mountains of Israel, in the valleys and in all the inhabited places of the country." 13

"I will feed them in good pasture, and their fold shall be on the high mountains of Israel. There shall they lie down in A Good Fold and feed in rich pasture on the mountains of Israel." 14 "I will feed My Flock, and I will make them lie down," says The Lord God. 15 "I will seek what was lost and bring back what was driven away, bind up the broken and strengthen what was sick; but I will destroy the fat and the strong, and feed them in Judgment." 16

"Therefore as I Live," says The Lord God, "I will do according to your anger and according to your envy which you showed in your hatred against them; and I will make Myself known among them when I Judge You" (35:11). "Then you shall know that I Am The Lord. I have heard all your blasphemies which you have spoken against the mountains of Israel, saying, 'They are desolate; they are given to us to consume.'" 12 "Thus with your mouth you have boasted against Me and multiplied your words against Me; I have heard them." 13 Thus says The Lord God: "The whole earth will rejoice when I make you desolate." 14

Seek good and not evil, that you may live; so The Lord God of hosts will be with you, as you have spoken (Amos 5:14). Hate evil, love good; establish Justice in the gate. It may be that The Lord God of hosts will be gracious to The Remnant of Joseph. 15 Therefore The Lord God of hosts, The Lord, says This: "There will be wailing in all streets, and they shall say in all the highways, 'Alas! Alas!' They shall call the farmer to mourning, and skillful lamenters to wailing. 16 In all your vineyards there shall be wailing, for I will pass through you," says The Lord. 17

Then The Angel of The Lord answered and said, "O Lord of hosts, how long will You not have mercy on Jerusalem and on The Cities of Judah, against which You were angry these 'seventy years'?" (Zech. 1:12). So the angel who spoke with me said to me, "Proclaim, saying, 'Thus says

The Lord of hosts: "I Am zealous for Jerusalem and for Zion with great zeal. 14 I Am exceedingly angry with the nations at ease; for I was a little angry, and they helped—but with evil intent." 15 "Therefore thus says The Lord: I Am returning to Jerusalem with mercy; My House shall be built in it," says The Lord of hosts, "and a surveyor's line shall be stretched out over Jerusalem." 16

Woe to those who devise iniquity, and work out evil on their beds! At morning light they practice it, because it is in the power of their hand (Micah 2:1). They covet fields and take them by violence, also houses, and seize them. So they oppress a man and his house, a man and his inheritance. 2 Therefore thus says The Lord: "Behold, against this family I am devising disaster, from which you cannot remove your necks, nor shall you walk haughtily, for This is an evil time. 3 In 'That Day' One shall take up a proverb against you, and lament with a bitter lamentation, saying: 'We are utterly destroyed! He has changed The Heritage of My People; He has removed it from me! To a turncoat He has divided our fields.'" 4 Therefore you will have no one to determine boundaries by lot in The Assembly of The Lord. 5

You who are named The House of Jacob: "Is The Spirit of The Lord restricted? Are these His Doings? Do not My Words do good to him who walks Uprightly?" 7 "Arise and depart, for this is not your rest; because it is defiled, it shall destroy, yes, with utter destruction." 10 "I will surely assemble All of you, O Jacob, I will surely gather The Remnant of Israel; I will put them together like sheep of a fold, like a flock in the midst of their pasture; they shall make a loud noise because of so many people." 12

But truly I Am full of power by The Spirit of The Lord, and of justice and might, to declare to Jacob his transgression and to Israel his sin

(Micah 3:8). Now hear this, you heads of The House of Jacob and rulers of The House of Israel, who abhor justice and pervert all equity, 9 Who build up Zion with bloodshed and Jerusalem with iniquity: 10 Her heads judge for a bribe, her priests teach for pay, and her prophets divine for money. Yet they lean on The Lord, and say, "Is not The Lord among us? No harm can come upon us." 11 Now why do you cry aloud? Is there no king in your midst? Has your counselor perished? For pangs have seized you like a woman in labor (4:9).

But they do not know The Thoughts of The Lord, nor do they understand His Counsel; for He Will Gather Them like sheaves to the threshing floor. 12 "But you, Bethlehem Ephrathah, though you are little among thousands of Judah, yet out of you Shall Come Forth to Me 'The One' to be ruler in Israel, who goings forth are from of old, from everlasting" (5:2). And He Shall Stand and feed His Flock in The Strength of The Lord, in The Majesty of The Name of The Lord His God; and They Shall Abide, for now He Shall be great to the ends of the earth; 4

And The Remnant of Jacob shall be among the Gentiles, in the midst of many people, like a lion among the beast of the forest, like a young lion among the flocks of sheep, who, if he passes through, both treads down and tears in pieces, and none shall deliver. 8 "And it shall be in That Day," says The Lord, "That I will cut off your horses from your midst and destroy your chariots. 10 I will cut off the cities of your land and throw down all your strongholds. 11 I will cut off sorceries from your hand, and you shall have no soothsayers. 12 Your carved images I will also cut off, and your sacred pillars from your midst; you shall no more worship the works of your hands; 13 I will pluck your wooden images from your midst; thus I will destroy your cities. 14 And I will execute vengeance in anger and fury on the nations that have not heard." 15

The Lord's Voice cries to the city—Wisdom shall see your name: "Hear the rod! Who has appointed it?" (6:9). Are there yet the treasures of wickedness in the house of the wicked, and the short measure that is an abomination? 10 Shall I count pure those with the wicked scales, and with the bags of deceitful weights? 11 For the rich men are full of violence, her inhabitants have spoken lies, and their tongue is deceitful in their mouth. 12 "Therefore I will also make you sick by striking you, by making you desolate because of your sins." 13

Behold, The Lord's Hand is not shortened, that It cannot save; nor His ear heavy, that It cannot hear (Isa. 59:1). But your iniquities have separated you from Your God; and your sins have hidden His Face from you, so that He will not hear. 2 For your hands are defiled with blood, and your fingers with iniquity; your lips have spoken lies, your tongue has muttered perversity. 3 No one calls for justice, nor does any plead for Truth. They trust in empty words and speak lies; they conceive evil and bring forth iniquity. 4 Their feet run to evil, and they make haste to shed innocent blood; their thoughts are thoughts of iniquity; wasting and destruction are in their paths. 7 The Way of Peace they have not known, and there is no justice in their ways; they have made themselves crooked paths; whoever takes that way shall not know peace. 8

According to their deeds, accordingly He will repay, fury to His adversaries, recompense to His enemies; the coastlands He will fully repay. 18 So shall they fear The Name of The Lord from the west, and His Glory from The Rising of The Sun; when the enemy comes in like a flood, The Spirit of The Lord will lift up a standard. 19 "The Redeemer will come to Zion, and to those who turn from transgression in Jacob," says The Lord. 20

For all those things My Hand has made, and all those things exist, says The Lord, "But on This One will I look: on him who is poor and of A Contrite Spirit, and who trembles at My Word" (66:2). Hear The Word of The Lord, you who tremble at His Word: "Your brethren who hated you, who cast you out for My Name's Sake, said, 'Let The Lord be Glorified, that they may see your joy.' But they shall be ashamed." 5 The sound of noise from the city! A Voice from the temple! The Voice of The Lord, who fully repays His enemies! 6

Then Jesus answered and said to them, "Most assuredly I say to you, The Son can do nothing of Himself, but what He see The Father do; for whatever He does, The Son also does in like manner" (John 5:19). "For The Father loves The Son, and shows Him all things that He Himself does; and He will show Him greater works then these, that you may marvel. 20 "For as The Father raises the dead, and gives Life to them, even so The Son gives Life to whom He will." 21 "Most assuredly, I say to you, he who hears My Word and believes in Him who sent Me has Everlasting Life, and shall not come into judgment, but has passed from death into Life." 24 "I can of Myself do nothing, As I hear, I judge; and My Judgment is Righteous, because I do not seek My own will but The Will of The Father who sent Me." 30

Therefore I have reason to glory in Christ Jesus in the things which pertain to God (Rom. 15:17). For I will not dare to speak of any of those things which Christ has not accomplished through Me, in Word and Deed, to make the Gentiles obedient. 18 In mighty signs, and wonders, by The Power of The Spirit of God, so that from Jerusalem and round about to Illyricum I have fully preached The Gospel of Christ. 19 Now I urge you, brethren, note those who cause divisions and offenses, contrary to The Doctrine which you learned, and avoid them (16:17). For those who are such do not serve our Lord Jesus Christ, but their own belly, and by smooth words and flattering speech deceive the heart of the simple. 18 For your obedience has become known to all. Therefore I am glad on your behalf; but I want you be wise in what is good, and simple concerning evil. 19

For Jerusalem stumbled, and Judah is fallen, because their tongue and their doings are against The Lord, to provoke The Eyes of His Glory (Isa. 3:8). The look of their countenance witnesses against them, and they declare their sin as Sodom; they do not hide it. Woe to their soul! For they have brought evil upon themselves. 9 Woe to the wicked! It shall be ill with him, for the reward of his hands shall be given him. 11 Woe to those who call evil good, and good evil; who put darkness for light, and light for darkness; who put bitter for sweet, and sweet for bitter! (5:20). Woe to those who are wise in their own eyes, and prudent in their own sight! 21 Woe to men mighty at drinking wine, woe to men valiant for mixing intoxicating drink, 22 Who justify the wicked for a bribe, and take away justice from the righteous man! 23

"Woe to those who decree unrighteous decrees, who write misfortune, which they have prescribed" (Isa. 10:1). To rob the needy of justice, and to take what is right from the poor of My people, that widows may be their prey, and that they may rob the fatherless. 2 What will you do in The Day of Punishment, and in the desolation which will come from afar? To whom will you flee for help? And where will you leave your glory? 3 For The Lord God of hosts will make A Determined End in the midst of all the land. 23 "I will punish the world for its evil, and the wicked for their iniquity; I will halt the arrogance of the proud, and will lay low the haughtiness of the terrible" (13:11).

This I say, therefore, and testify in The Lord, that you should no longer walk as the rest of the Gentiles walk, in the futility of their mind (Eph.

4:17). Having their understanding darkened, being alienated from The Life of God, because of the ignorance that is in them, because of the blindness of their heart; 18 Who, being past feeling, have given themselves over to lewdness, to work all uncleanness with greediness. 19 But you have not so learned Christ, 20 If indeed you have heard Him and have been taught by Him, as The Truth is in Jesus: 21 That you put off, concerning your former conduct, The old man which grows corrupt according to the deceitful lusts, 23 And that you put on "The New Man" which was Created according to God, in True Righteousness and Holiness.

And He said to Me, "Son of man, stand on your feet, and I will speak to You" (Ezek. 2:1). Then The Spirit entered Me when He spoke to Me, and set me on My feet; and I heard Him who spoke to Me. 2 And He said to Me: "Son of man, I Am sending You to The Children of Israel, to A Rebellious Nation that has rebelled against Me; they and their fathers have transgressed against Me to This Very Day." 3 "For they are impudent and stubborn children. I Am sending You to them, and You shall say to them, 'Thus says The Lord God.' 4 As for them, whether they will hear or whether they refuse—for they are A Rebellious House—yet they will know that a prophet has been among them. 5 Then He said to Me: "Son of man, go to The House of Israel and speak My Words to them" (3:4).

Hear The Word of The Lord, you Children of Israel, for The Lord brings A Charge against the inhabitants of the land: "There is no Truth or Mercy or Knowledge of God in the land" (Hosea 4:1). "By swearing and lying, killing and stealing and committing adultery, they break all restraint, with bloodshed upon bloodshed." 2 "The more they increased, the more they sinned against Me; I will change their glory into shame." 7 "My people ask counsel from their wooden idols, and their staff informs them, For the spirit of harlotry has caused them to stray, and they have played the harlot against their God."12 Their drink is rebellion, they commit harlotry continually. Her ruler dearly love dishonor. 18 "They do not direct their deeds toward turning to their God, for the spirit of harlotry is in their midst, and they do not 'Know The Lord.'" (5:4). They have dealt treacherously with The Lord, for they have begotten pagan children. Now a New Moon shall devour them and their heritage. 7

Let us know, let us pursue The Knowledge of The Lord. His going forth is established as the morning; He will come to us like the rain, like the latter and former rain to the earth (6:3). Therefore I have hewn them by the prophets, I have slain them by The Word of My Mouth; and Your Judgment are like Light that goes forth. 5 For I desire Mercy and not sacrifice, and The Knowledge of God more than burnt offerings. 6 And the pride of Israel testifies to his face, but they do not return to The Lord their God, nor Seek Him for all This (7:10). "They sow the wind, and reap the whirlwind. The stalk has no bud; it shall never produce meal. If it should produce, aliens would swallow it up" (8:7).

Brethren, My heart's desire and prayer to God for Israel is that they may be saved (Rom. 10:1). For I bear them witness that they have the Zeal. of God, but not according to Knowledge. 2 For they being ignorant of God's Righteousness, and seeking to establish their own righteousness, have not submitted to The Righteousness of God. 3 For Christ is the end of The Law for righteousness to everyone who Believes. 4

For it is The God who commanded Light to shine out of darkness, who has shone in our hearts to give The Light of Knowledge of The Glory of God in The Face of Jesus Christ (2 Cor. 4:6). Knowing, therefore, The Terror of The Lord, we persuade men; but we are well known to God, and I trust are well known in your conscience (5:11). For if we are beside ourselves, it is for God; or if we are of sound mind, it is for you. 13 Now all things are of God, who has reconciled us to Himself through Jesus Christ, and has given us The Ministry of Reconciliation. 18 Now then, we are Ambassadors for Christ, as though God were pleading through us: We Implore You on Christ's Behalf, be reconciled to God. 20

We then, as workers together with Him also plead with you not to receive The Grace of God in vain (6:1). For He says: "In an acceptable time I have heard you, and in The Day of Salvation I have helped you." "Behold, Now is 'The Accepted Time'; Behold, Now is 'The Day of Salvation.'" 2 Therefore, although I wrote to you, I did not do it for the sake of him who has done the wrong, nor for the sake of him who suffered wrong, but for our care for you in The Sight of God might appear to you (7:12).

"Behold, The eyes of The Lord God are on The Sinful Kingdom, and I will destroy it from The Face of The Earth; yet I will not utterly destroy The House of Jacob," says The Lord (Amos 9:8). "For surely I will command, and will sift The House of Israel among all nations, as grain is sifted in a sieve; yet not the smallest grain shall fall to the ground." 9 All the sinners of My People shall die by The Sword, who say, 'The calamity shall not overtake nor confront us.'" 10 "On 'That Day' I will raise up The Tabernacle of David, which has fallen down, and repair its damages; I will raise up its ruins, and rebuild it as in The Days of Old; 11 That they may possess The Remnant of Edom, and all the Gentiles who are Called by My Name," says The Lord who does 'This Thing.'" 12

Then Peter opened his mouth and said: "In Truth I perceive that God shows no partiality" (Acts 10:34). "But in every nation whoever fears

Him and works righteousness is accepted by Him" 35 "The Word which God sent to The Children of Israel, preaching peace through Jesus Christ—He is Lord of All." 36 "That Word you know, which was proclaimed throughout all Judea, and began from Galilee after The Baptism which John preached: 37 How God anointed Jesus of Nazareth with The Holy Spirit and with power, and who went about doing good and healing all who were oppressed by the devil, for God was with Him. 38 And we are witnesses of all things which He did both in the land of the Jews and in Jerusalem, whom they killed by hanging on a tree. 39 Him God raised up on the third day and showed Him openly." 40 "And He commanded us to preach to the people, and to testify that it is He who was Ordained of God to be Judge of the living and the dead." 42 "Then he said, 'The God of our fathers has Chosen You that you should know His Will, and see The Just One, and hear The Voice of His Mouth'" (22:14). "For you will be His Witness to All Men of what you have seen and heard." 15

Blessed be The God and Father of our Lord Jesus Christ, who according to His Abundant Mercy has Begotten Us Again to "A Living Hope" through The Resurrection of Jesus Christ from the dead (1 Pet. 1:3). To an inheritance incorruptible and undefiled and that does not "Fade Away," reserved in heaven for you, 4 Who are kept by The Power of God through faith for Salvation ready to be revealed In The Last Time. 5 Of This Salvation the prophets have inquired and searched carefully, who prophesied of The Grace that would come to you, 10

Therefore The Lord says, The Lord of hosts, The Mighty One of Israel, "Ah, I will rid Myself of My adversaries, and take vengeance on My enemies" (Isa. 1:24). I will turn My Hand against you, and thoroughly purge away your dross, and take away all your alloy. 25 I will "Restore" your judges as at The First, and your counselors as at The Beginning.

Afterward you shall be called "The City of Righteousness," The faithful City. 26 Zion shall be "Redeemed" with justice, and her penitents with Righteousness. 27

Many people shall "Come" and say, "Come, and let us go up to The Mountain of The Lord, to The House of The God of Jacob; He will teach us 'His Ways,' and we will walk in 'His Paths.'" For out of Zion shall go forth 'The Law,' and The Word of The Lord from Jerusalem (2:3). He shall judge between nations, and rebuke many people; they shall beat their swords into plowshares, and their spears into pruning hooks; nation shall not lift up sword against nation, neither shall they learn war anymore. 4

The lofty looks of man shall be humbled, the haughtiness of men shall be bowed down, and The Lord alone shall be "Exalted in That Day." 11 For The Day of The Lord of hosts shall come upon every proud and lofty, upon everything lifted up—and it shall be brought down. 12 For Jerusalem stumbled, and Judah is fallen, because their tongue and their doings are against The Lord, to provoke The Eyes of His Glory (3:8). But The Lord of hosts shall be "Exalted in Judgment," and God Who is Holy shall be "Hallowed in Righteousness" (5:16). For The Lord God of hosts will make "A Determined End" in the midst of all the land (10:23). He will set up "A Banner" for the nations, and will "Assemble" The Outcasts of Israel, and "Gather Together" The Dispersed of Judah from The Four Corners of The Earth (11:12). "Cry Out and Shout, O Inhabitants of Zion, for Great is The Holy One of Israel in your midst!" (12:6). What will they answer The Messengers of The Nation? That The Lord has founded Zion, and the poor of His People shall take "Refuge in It" (14:32).

Then The Word of The Lord came to Me saying (Jer. 1:4). "Before I formed you in the womb 'I Knew You'; before You were born 'I Sanctified You'; 'I Ordained You' a prophet to the nations." 5 Then The Lord put forth His Hand and touched My Mouth, and The Lord said to Me: "Behold, I have put My Words in Your mouth. 9 See, I have 'This Day' set You over the nations and over the kingdoms, to root out and to pull down, to destroy and to throw down, to build and to plant." 10 "For behold, I have made You 'This Day' a fortified city and an iron pillar, and bronze walls against the whole land—against the kings of Judah, against its princes, against its priest, and against the people of the land." 18

"Have you not brought 'This' on yourself, in that you have forsaken The Lord your God when He led you in 'The Way'?" 17 "Your own wickedness will correct you, and your backsliding will rebuke you. Know therefore and see that it is an evil and bitter thing that you have forsaken The Lord your God, and 'The Fear of Me' is not in you, says The Lord God of hosts. 19 Listen!" "The Voice," the cry of The Daughter of My People from a far country: "Is not The Lord in Zion? Is not Her King in her?" "Why have they provoked Me to anger with their carved images—with foreign idols?" (8:19). "For The Lord of hosts, who planted you, has pronounced doom against you for the evil of The House of Israel and of The House of Judah, which they have done against themselves to provoke Me to anger in offering incense to Baal" (11:17).

O Lord, You know; remember Me and visit Me, and take vengeance for Me on My persecutors. In Your enduring patience, do not take Me away. Know for Your Sake I have suffered rebuke (15:15). You Words were found, and I ate them, and Your Word was to Me The Joy and Rejoicing of My Heart; for I Am called by Your Name, O Lord God of hosts. 16 I did not sit in the assembly of the mockers, nor did I rejoice; I set alone because of Your Hand, for You have filled Me with indignation. 17

"Behold, I will send for many Fishermen," says The Lord, "and they shall fish them; and afterward I will send for many hunters, and they shall hunt them from every mountain and every hill, and out of the holes of the rocks" (16:16). For My Eyes are on all their ways, they are not hidden from My Face, nor is their iniquity hidden from My Eyes. 17 "And first I will repay double for their iniquity and their sin, because they have defiled My Land, they have filled My Inheritance with the carcasses of their detestable and abominable idols. 18 Thus says The Lord: 'Cursed is the man who trusts in man and makes flesh his strength, whose heart departs from The Lord (17:5). O Lord, The Hope of Israel, all who forsake You shall be ashamed. Those who depart from Me shall be written in the earth, because they have forsaken The Lord, The Fountain of Living Waters.'" 13

"The instant I speak concerning a nation and concerning a kingdom, to pluck up, to pull down, and to destroy it" (18:7). If that nation against whom I have spoken turns from evil, I will relent of the disaster that I thought to bring upon it." 8

"And the instant I speak concerning a nation and concerning a kingdom, to build and to plant it, 9 If it does evil in My Sight so that it does not obey My Voice, then I will relent concerning the good with which I said I would benefit it." 10 "Now therefore, speak to The Men of Judah and to The inhabitants of Jerusalem, saying, 'Thus says The Lord: "Behold, I Am fashioning A Disaster and devising A Plan against you. Return Now everyone from his evil way, and make your ways and your doings good." 11 "Because My People have forgotten Me, they have burned incense to worthless idols. And they have caused themselves to stumble in their ways, from The Ancient Paths, to walk in pathways and not on a highway, 15 To make their land desolate and a perpetual hissing; everyone who passes by it will be astonished and shake their head." 16

"Thus says The Lord: Execute Judgment and Righteousness, and deliver the plundered out of the hand of the oppressor. Do no wrong and do no violence to the stranger, the fatherless, or the widow, nor shed innocent blood in This Place'" (22:3). "For if you indeed do This Thing, then shall enter the gates of This House, riding on horses and in chariots, accompanied by servants and people, Kings who sit on The Throne of David. 4 "Therefore 'The Days are Coming,' says The Lord, 'that they shall no longer say, As The Lord lives who brought up The Children of Israel from the land of Egypt'" (23:7). "But, 'As The Lord Lives who brought up and led The Descendants of The House of Israel from the north country and from all the countries where I have driven them.' And they shall dwell in their own land." 8

My heart within Me is broken because of the prophets; all My bones shake. I am like a drunken man, and like a man whom wine has overcome, because of The Lord, and because of His Holy Words. 9 For the land is full of adulterers; for because of A Curse the land mourns. The pleasant places of the wilderness are dried up. Their course of Life is evil, and their might is not right. 10 "For both prophet and priest are profane; yes, in My House I have found their wickedness," says The Lord. 11 "Therefore their way shall be to them like slippery ways; in the darkness they shall be driven on and fall in them; for I will bring disaster on them, The Year of Their Punishment," says The Lord. 12 "Is not My Word like a fire? says The Lord, "and like a hammer that breaks the rock in pieces?" 29

"If there arises among you a prophet or a dreamer of dreams, and he gives you a sign or a wonder" (Deut. 13:1). "And the sign or the wonder comes to pass, of which he spoke to you, saying, 'Let us go after other gods'—which you have not known—and let us serve them.'" 2 "You shall not listen to the words of that prophet or that dreamer of dreams, for The Lord God is testing you to know whether you love The Lord your God, with all your heart and with all your soul." 3 "You shall walk after The Lord your God and fear Him, and keep His Commandments and obey His Voice; you shall serve Him and hold fast to Him" 4 "For you are A Holy People to The Lord your God, and The Lord has chosen you to be A People for Himself, A Special Treasure above all the peoples who are on the face of the earth" (14:2).

"Is the iniquity of Peor not enough for us, from which we are not cleansed till 'This Day,' although there was a plague in The Congregation of the Lord" (Josh. 22:17). "Therefore be very courageous to keep and to do all that is written in The Book of The Law of Moses, lest you turn aside from it to the right hand or to the left" (23:6). "Therefore take careful heed to yourselves, that you love The Lord your God." 11 "Now therefore, Fear The Lord, serve Him in sincerity and in Truth, and put away the gods which your fathers served on the other side of the River and in Egypt. Serve The Lord!" (24:14).

Then King David went in and sat before The Lord; and he said: "Who am I, O Lord God? And what is My House, that You have brought Me this far?" (1 Chron. 17:16). "And yet this is a small thing in Your Sight, O God; and You have spoken of Your servant's House for a great while to come, and have regarded Me according to the rank of a man of high degree, O Lord God." 17 "What more can David say to You for the honor of Your servant? For You know Your servant. 18 "O Lord, for Your servant's sake, and according to Your own heart, You

have done all this greatness, in making known all these great things."
19 "O Lord, there is none like You, nor is there any God beside You,
according to all that we have heard with our ears." 20 "And who is like
Your People Israel, the one nation on the earth whom God went to
redeem for Himself as a people—to make for Yourself a name by great
and awesome deeds, by driving out nations from before Your people
whom You redeemed from Egypt?" 21

"For You have made Your People Israel Your very own people forever;
and You, Lord, have become their God." 22 "And Now, O Lord, The
Word which You have spoken concerning Your servant and concerning
His House, let it be established forever, and do as You have said." 23
"So let it be established, that Your Name may be magnified forever,
saying, 'The Lord of hosts, The God of Israel, is Israel's God.' And let
The House of Your Servant David be established before you." 24 "For
You, O My God, have revealed to Your servant that You will build
him A House. Therefore Your servant has found in His Heart to Pray
Before You." 25 "And Now, Lord, You are God, and have promised This
Goodness to Your servant." 26 "Now You have been pleased to bless The
House of Your servant, that it may continue before You forever; for You
have blessed it, O Lord, and it shall be blessed forever." 27

"Let all the nations be gathered together, and let The People be
assembled. Who among them can declare 'This,' and show us former
things? Let them bring out their witnesses, that they may be justified;
or let them hear and say, 'IT IS TRUTH.'" (Isa. 43:10).

Jesus said to him, "I Am 'The Way,' 'The Truth' and 'The Life.' No one
comes to The Father except through Me" (John 14:6). "And I will pray
The Father, and He will give you another Helper, That He may abide
with you forever."16 "The Spirit of Truth," whom the world cannot

receive, because it neither sees Him nor knows Him; but you know Him, for He dwells with you and will be in you. 17 "But The Helper, The Holy Spirit, whom The Father will send in My Name. He will teach you all things, and bring to your remembrance all things that I said to you." 26 "And when He has come. He will convict the world of sin, and of righteousness, and of judgment" (16:8). Of sin, because they do not believe in Me; 9 Of righteousness, because I go to My Father and you see Me know more; 10 Of judgment, because the rulers of this world is judged. 11 However when He, The Spirit of Truth, has come, He will guide you into all Truth; for He will not speak on His own authority, but whatever He hears He Will Speak; and He will tell you things to come. 13

"Men Of Israel, Hear These Words: Jesus of Nazareth, A Man attested by God to you by miracles, wonders, and signs which God did through Him in your midst, as you yourselves also know" (Acts 2:22). "Him, being delivered by 'The Determined Purpose' and foreknowledge of God, you have taken by lawless hands, have crucified, and put to death" 23 "Whom God raised up, having loosed the pains of death, because it was possible that He should be held by it." 24 "This Jesus God has raised up, of which we are all witnesses." 32 "Therefore being exalted to The Right Hand of God, and having received from The Father 'The Promise of The Holy Spirit,' He poured out 'This' which you 'Now See and Hear.'" 33 "For 'The Promise' is to you and to your children, and to all who are afar off, as many as The Lord our God will 'Call.'" 39

"Then He said, 'The God of our fathers 'Has Chosen You' that you should know 'His Will,' and see The Just One, and hear The Voice of His Mouth" (22:14). "For you will be His Witness to all men of what you have seen and heard" 15 "The Lord gives Voice before His Army, for His Camp is very great; for strong is 'The One' who executes His

Word. For 'The Day of The Lord' is great and very terrible; who can endure it?" (Joel 2:11). "Now therefore," says The Lord, "Turn to Me with all your heart, with fasting, with weeping, and with mourning." 12 So rend your heart, and not your garments; Return to The Lord your God, for He is gracious and merciful, slow to anger, and of great kindness; and He relents from doing harm. 13

Blow "The Trumpet" in Zion, consecrate a fast, Call "A Sacred Assembly"; 15 Gather The People, sanctify the congregation, assemble the elders, gather the children and nursing babes; let The Bridegroom go out from His Chamber, and The Bride from her dressing room. 16 Then The Lord will be zealous for His Land, and pity His People. 18 The Lord will answer and say to His People, "Behold, I will send you grain and new wine and oil, and you will be satisfied by them; I will no longer make you a reproach among the nations. 19 Through The Lord's Mercies we are not consumed, because His Compassions fail not" (Lam. 3:22). The Lord is good to those who wait for Him, to the those who seeks Him. 25 For The Lord will not cast off forever. 31 Though He causes grief, yet He will show compassion according to The Multitude of His Mercies. 32 All our enemies have opened their mouth against us. 46 Fear and a snare have come upon us, desolation and destruction. 47 Our inheritance has been turned over to aliens, and our houses to foreigners (5:2). Because of This our heart is faint; because of These Things our eyes grow dim. 17

Then The King turned around and blessed The Whole Assembly of Israel, while all The Assembly of Israel was standing (2 Chron. 6:3). And He said: "Blessed be The Lord God of Israel, who hath fulfilled with His Hands what 'He Spoke' with His Mouth to my father David, saying, 4 'Since the day that I brought My People out of The Land of Egypt, I have chosen no city from any tribe of Israel in which to build A House, that

My Name might be there, nor did I choose any man to be A Ruler over My People Israel. 5 Yet I have chosen Jerusalem, that My Name may be there, and I have chosen David to be over My People Israel.'" 6 "Now it was in The Heart of My Father David to build a temple for The Name of The Lord God of Israel." 7 "But The Lord said to my father David, 'Whereas it was in your heart to build a temple for My Name, you did well in that it was in your heart. 8 Nevertheless you shall not build the temple, but the son that comes from your body, he shall build The Temple for My Name Sake.'" 9 "So The Lord has fulfilled His Word which He Spoke, and I have filled The Position of my father David, and sit of The Throne of Israel, as The Lord Promised; and I have built The Temple for The Name of The Lord God of Israel." 10

And he said: "Lord God of Israel, there is no God in heaven or on earth like You, who keep Your Covenant and Mercy with Your Servants who walk before You with all their hearts." 14 "You have kept what You Promised Your Servant David my father; You have spoken with Your Mouth and fulfilled it with Your Hands, at it is 'This Day.'" 15 "Therefore, Lord God of Israel, now keep what You Promised Your Servant David my father, saying, 'You shall not fail to have a man sit before Me on The Throne of Israel, only if your sons take heed to their way, that they may Walk in My Law as you have walked before Me.'" 16 "And now, O Lord God of Israel, let Your Word come true, which You have spoken to Your Servant David." 17 "But will God indeed dwell with man on the earth? Behold, heaven and the heavens of heavens cannot contain You. How much less this temple which I have built!"

"Yet regard The Prayer of Your Servant and his supplication, O Lord My God, and listen to the cry and the prayer which Your Servant is praying before You." 19 "That Your Eyes may be open toward This Temple day and night, toward the place where You Said You would put Your Name, that You may hear the prayer which Your Servant makes toward This Place." 20 "And may You hear the supplications of Your Servant and of Your People Israel, when they pray toward This Place. Hear from heaven Your dwelling place, and when You hear, FORGIVE." 21

"If anyone sins against his neighbor, and is forced to take an oath, and comes and takes an oath before Your altar in This Temple, 22 Then hear from heaven, and act, and judge Your Servants, bringing retribution on the wicked by bringing his way on his own head, and Justifying The Righteous by giving him according to his righteousness." 23 "Or if Your People Israel are defeated before an enemy because they have sinned against You, and Return and Confess Your Name, and pray and make supplication before You in This Temple, 24 Then hear from heaven and Forgive the sin of Your people Israel, and bring them back to the land which You gave them and their fathers." 25

"When the heavens are shut up and there is no rain because they have sinned against You, when they pray toward This Place and Confess Your Name, and turn from their sin because You afflict them, 26 Then hear from heaven, and Forgive the sin of Your Servant, Your People Israel, that You may teach them 'The Good Way' in which they should walk; and send rain on Your Land which You have given to Your People as an inheritance." 27

"When there is famine in the land, pestilence or blight or mildew, locusts or grasshoppers; when their enemies besiege them in the land of their cities; whatever plague or whatever sickness there is; 28 Whatever prayer, whatever supplication is made by anyone, or by All Your People Israel, when each one knows his own burden and his own grief, and spread out his hands to This Temple: 29 Then hear from heaven Your Dwelling Place, and Forgive, and give to everyone according to all his ways, whose heart You Know (For You alone know the hearts of the sons of men), 30 That they may Fear You, to walk in Your Ways as long as they live in The Land which You gave to their fathers." 31

"Moreover, concerning a foreigner, who is not of Your people Israel, but has come from a far country for The Sake of Your Great Name and Your Mighty Hand and Your outstretched arm, when they come and pray in This Temple; 32 Then hear from heaven Your Dwelling Place, and do according for which the foreigner calls to You, that all peoples of the earth may Know Your Name and Fear You, as do Your People Israel, and that they may know that This Temple which I have built is called by Your Name." 33

"When Your People go out to battle against their enemies, wherever You send them, and when they pray to You toward This City which You Have Chosen and The Temple which You have built for Your Name. 33 Then hear from heaven their prayer and their supplication, and maintain Their Cause. 35 When they sin against You (For there is no one who does not sin), and You become angry with them and deliver them to the enemy, and they take them captive to a land far or near; 36 Yet when they come to themselves in the land they where they were carried captive, and Repent, and make supplication to You in the land of their captivity, saying, 'We have sinned, we have done wrong, and have committed wickedness; 37 And when they Return to You with all their heart and with all their soul in the land of their captivity, where they have been carried captive, and pray toward their land which you gave to their fathers, The City which You Have Chosen, and toward The Temple which I have built for Your Name: 38 Then hear from heaven Your Dwelling Place their prayer and their supplications, and maintain their cause, and forgive Your People who have sinned against You." 39

"Now, My God, I pray, let Your eyes be open and let Your ears be attentive to The Prayer made in This Place. 40

Now therefore, Arise, O Lord God, to Your Resting Place, You and The Ark of Your Strength. Let Your priests, O Lord God, be clothed with Salvation, and let Your Saints rejoice in Goodness. 41 O Lord God, do not turn away The Face of Your Anointed; remember The Mercies of Your Servant David. 42

Then The Lord appeared to Solomon by night, and said to him: "I have heard your prayer and have chosen This Place for Myself as A House of Sacrifice (7:12). When I shut up heaven and there is no rain, or command the locusts to devour the land or send pestilence among My People, 13 If My People who are called by My Name will humble themselves, and pray and seek My Face, and turn from their wicked ways, then I will hear from heaven, and will forgive their sin and heal their land. 14 Now My eyes will be open and My ears attentive to prayer made in This Place. For now I have Chosen and Sanctified This House, that My Name may be there forever; and My eyes and My heart will be there perpetually." 16

"As for you, if you walk before Me as your father David walk, and do according to all that I commanded you, and if you keep My Statutes and My Judgments, 17 Then I will establish The Throne of Your Kingdom, as I covenanted with David your father, saying, 'You shall not fail to have a man as Ruler in Israel.' 18 But if you turn away and forsake My Statutes and My Commandments which I have sit before you, and go and serve other gods, and worship them, 19 Then I will uproot them from My Land which I have given them; and This House which I have sanctified for My Name I will cast out of My sight, and will make it a proverb and a byword among all peoples." 20

"And as for This House, which is exalted, everyone who passes by it will be astonished and say, 'Why has The Lord done thus to This Land and This House?' 21 Then you will answer, 'Because they forsook The Lord God of their fathers, who brought them out of the land of Egypt, and embraced other gods, and worshiped them and served them; therefore He has brought all this calamity on them.'" 22

"How have you helped him who is without power? How have you saved the arm that had no strength?" (Job 26:2). "How have you counseled one who has no wisdom? And how have you declared sound advice to many? 3 To whom have you uttered words? And whose spirit came from you? 4 Indeed these are the mere edges of His Ways, and how small of whisper we hear of Him! But the thunder of His Power who can understand?" 14

"As God Lives, who has taken away my justice, and The Almighty, who has made my soul bitter" (27:2). "As long as my breath is in me, and The Breath of God in my nostrils, 3 My lips will not speak wickedness, nor my tongue utter deceit. 4 For what is The Hope of The Hypocrite, though he may gain much, if God takes away his Life? 8 Will God hear his cry when trouble comes upon him? 9 Will he delight himself in The Almighty? Will he always call on God? 10 I will teach you about The Hand of God; what is with The Almighty I Will Not Conceal. 11 Surely all of you have seen it; why then do you behave with complete nonsense?" 12

"This is the portion of a wicked man with God, and the heritage of the oppressor, received from The Almighty: 13 If his children are multiplied, it is for the sword; and his offspring shall not be satisfied with bread. 14 Those who survive him shall be buried in death, and their widows will not weep, 15 Though he heaps up silver like dust, and piles up clothing like clay." 16 He may pile it up, but The Just will wear it, and The Innocent will divide the silver." 17

But where can wisdom be found? And where is the place of understanding? (28:12). "Man does not know its value, nor is it found in The Land of The Living. 13 The deep says, 'It is not in me'; and the sea says, 'It is not with me.' 14 God understands its way, and He knows it place. 23 And to man He Said, 'Behold, The Fear of The Lord, that is wisdom, and to depart from evil is understanding'" (28:28).

Turn at My Rebuke; surely I Will Pour out My Spirit on you; I Will Make 'My Words' known to you (Prov. 1:23). Because I Have Called and you refused, I Have Stretched out My Hand and no one regarded. 24 Because you disdained all My Counsel, and would have none of My Rebuke, 25 I also laugh at your calamity; I will mock when your terror comes, 26 But whoever listens to Me will dwell safely, and will be secure, without fear of evil. 33 When wisdom enters your heart, and knowledge is pleasant to your soul (2:10). Discretion will preserve you; understanding will keep you. 11 Do not be wise in your own eyes; Fear The Lord and Depart from evil (3:7).

Thus says The Lord of hosts, The God of Israel: "Amend your ways and your doings, and I will cause you to dwell in This Place" (Jer. 7:3). "Will you steal, murder, commit adultery, burn incense to Baal, and walk after other gods whom you do not know. 9 Do you not see what they do in the cities of Judah and in The Streets of Jerusalem?" 17 "But this is what I commanded them, saying, 'Obey My Voice, and I will be your God, and you shall be My People. And walk in all the ways that I commanded you, that it may be well with you.' 23 Yet they did not obey or incline their ear, but followed the counsels and the dictates of their evil hearts, and went backward and not forward." 24

"For The Children of Judah have done evil in My Sight," says The Lord. "They have set their abominations in The House which is called by My Name, to pollute it. 30 'Yet you have not listen to Me,' says The Lord, 'That you might provoke Me to anger with the works of your hands to you own hurt'" (25:7). A noise will come to The Ends of The Earth— for The Lord has a controversy with the nations; He will plead His Case with all flesh. He will give those who are wicked to The Sword. 31 "Perhaps everyone Will Listen and Turn from his evil way, that I may relent concerning The Calamity which I purpose to bring on them because of the evil of their doings" (26:3).

Now these are The Words that The lord spoke concerning Israel and Judah (30:4). "For Thus says The Lord: 'We have heard a voice of trembling, of fear, and not of peace. 5 Ask now, and see, whether a man is ever in labor with child? So why do I see every man with his hands on his loins like a woman in labor, and all faces turn pale? 6 Alas! For That Day is great, so that none is like it; and it is The Time of Jacob's Trouble, but he shall be saved out of it. 7 'For it shall come to pass in That Day,' says The Lord of hosts, 'That I will break his yoke from your neck, and will burst your bonds; foreigners shall no more enslave them. 8 But they shall serve The Lord their God, and David their king, whom I will raise up for them.'" 8

"Then shall the virgin rejoice in the dance, and the young men and the old, together; for I will turn their mourning to joy, will comfort them, and make them rejoice rather than sorrow" (31:13). "I will satiate the soul of the priests with abundance, and My People shall be satisfied with My Goodness, says The Lord." 14 "But this is The Covenant that I will make with The House of Israel after those days, says The Lord: I will put My Law in their minds, and write it on their hearts; and I will be their God, and they shall be My People. 33

"Ah, Lord God! Behold, You have made the heavens and the earth by Your Great Power and Outstretched Arm. There is nothing too hard for You" (32:17). "You show lovingkindness to thousands, and repay the iniquity of the father into the bosom of their children after them—The Great, The Mighty God, whose name is The Lord of hosts. 18 You are great in counsel and mighty in work, for Your Eyes are open to all the ways of The Son of Men, to give everyone according to his ways and according to the fruit of his doings. 19 You have set signs and wonders in the land of Egypt, to This Day, and in Israel and among other men; and You have made Yourself a name, as it is This Day. 20 You have brought Your People Israel out of the land of Egypt with signs and wonders, with A Strong Hand and Outstretched Arm, and with great terror; 21 You have given them This Land, of which You swore to their fathers to give them—a land flowing with milk and honey." 22

"Behold I will bring it health and healing; I will heal them and reveal to them The Abundance of Peace and Truth" (33:6). "And I will cause the captives of Judah and the captives of Israel to Return, and will rebuild those places as at the first. 7 I will cleanse them from all their iniquity by which they have sinned against Me, and I will pardon all their iniquities by which they have sinned and by which they have transgressed against Me. 8 In Those Days and at That Time I will cause to grow up to David A Branch of Righteousness; He shall execute Judgment and Righteousness in the earth." 15

"Declare among the nations, Proclaim, and set up a standard; Proclaim—do not conceal it—say, 'Babylon is taken, Bel is shamed. Merodach is broken in pieces; her idols are humiliated, her images are broken in pieces'" (50:2). For out of the north a nation comes up against her, which shall make her land desolate, and no one shall dwell therein. They shall move, they shall depart, both man and beast. 3 In

Those Days and in That Time, says The Lord, "The Children of Israel shall come, they and The Children of Judah together; with continual weeping they shall come, and Seek The Lord Their God. 4 They shall ask The Way to Zion, with their faces toward it, saying, Come and let us join ourselves to The Lord in A Perpetual Covenant that will not be forgotten." 5

My People have been lost sheep. Their shepherds have led them astray; they have turned them away on The Mountains. They have gone from mountain to hill, they have forgotten "Their Resting Place." 6 All who found them have devoured them; and their adversaries said, "We have not offended, because they have sinned against The Lord, The Habitation of Justice, The Lord, 'The Hope' of their fathers." 7 In Those Days and in That Time, says The Lord, "The iniquity of Israel shall be sought, but there shall be none; and the sins of Judah, but they shall not be found; for I Will Pardon those whom I Preserve." 20

The Lord has opened His Armory, and has brought out The Weapons of His Indignation; for "This" is The Work of The Lord God of hosts in the land of the Chaldeans. 25 Therefore her young men shall fall in the streets, and All her "Men of War" shall be cut off in That Day, says The Lord. 30 "Behold, I Am against you, O most haughty one!" says The Lord God of hosts; "For your day has come, The Time that I punish you." 31 "And I will repay Babylon and all the inhabitants of Chaldea for all the evil they have done in Zion in your sight," says The Lord (51:24).

For the idols speak delusion; the diviners envision lies, and tell false dreams; they comfort in vain. Therefore the people wend their way like sheep; they are in trouble because there is no shepherd (Zech. 10:2). "My anger is kindled against the shepherd, and I will punish the goatherds.

For The Lord of hosts will visit His Flock, The House of Judah, and will make them as His Royal Horse in the battle. 3 From him comes The Cornerstone, for him the tent peg, from him the battle bow, from him every ruler together. 4 They shall be like mighty men, who tread down their enemies in the mire of the streets in the battle. They shall fight because The Lord is with them, and the riders on horses shall be put to shame." 5

Thus says The Lord God: "Woe to the foolish prophets, who follow their own spirit and have seen nothing" (Ezek. 13:3). "Have you not seen a futile vision, and have you not spoken false divination? You say, 'The Lord says,' but I have not spoken." 7 "I will set My Face against that man and make him a sign and a proverb, and I will cut him off from the midst of My People. Then you shall know that I Am The Lord" (14:8). "And they shall bear their iniquity; The Punishment of the prophet shall be the same as The Punishment of the one who inquired, 10 That The House of Israel may no longer stray from Me, nor be profaned anymore with all their transgressions, but that they may be My People and I may be their God," says The Lord God. 11

In You, O Lord, I put my trust; let me never be put to shame (Ps. 71:1). Deliver me in Your Righteousness, and cause me to escape; incline Your Ear to me, and save me. 2 Be my strong refuge, to which I may resort continually; You have given the commandment to save me, for You are my Rock and my Fortress. 3 Deliver me, O my God, out of the hand of the wicked, out of the hand of the unrighteous and cruel man. 4 For You are My Hope, O Lord God; You are my trust from my youth. 5 By You I have been upheld from birth; You are He who took me out of my mother's womb. My praise shall be continually of You. 6

I have become a wonder to many, but You are My Strong Refuge. 7 Let my mouth be filled with Your Praise and with Your Glory all the day. 8 Do not cast me off in time of old age; do not forsake me when my strength fails. 9 For my enemies speak against me; and those who lie in wait for my life take counsel together. 10 Saying, "God has forsaken him; pursue and take him, for there is none to deliver." 11

O God, do not be far from me; O My God, make haste to help me! 12 Let them be confounded and consumed who are adversaries of My Life; let them be covered with reproach and dishonor who seek my hurt. 13 But I will hope continually, and will Praise You yet more and more. 14 My mouth shall tell of Your Righteousness and Your Salvation all the day, for I do not know their limits. 15 I will go in The Strength of The Lord God; I will make mention of Your Righteousness, of Yours Only. 16

O God, You have taught me from my youth; and to "This Day" I Declare Your Wondrous Works. 17 Now also when I am old and grayheaded, O God, do not forsake me, until "I Declare Your Strength" to This Generation, Your Power to "Everyone Who is to Come." 18 Also Your Righteousness, O God, is very high, You have done great things; O God, Who Is Like You? 19 You, who have shown me great and severe troubles, shall "Revive Me Again," and bring me up again from the depths of the earth. 20 You shall increase My Greatness, and Comfort Me on every side. 21 Also with the lute I will Praise You—and Your Faithfulness, O My God! to You I will sing with the harp, O Holy One of Israel. 22 My lips shall greatly rejoice when I Sing to You, and My Soul, which You Have Redeemed. 23 My tongue also shall talk of Your Righteousness all the day long; for they are confounded, for they are brought to shame who seek my hurt. 24 Fear and dread will fall on them; by The Greatness of Your Arm they will be still as a stone, till Your People Pass over, O Lord, till the people pass over whom You Have Purchased (Exod. 15:16). You will bring them in and plant them In The Mountain of Your Inheritance, in The Place, O Lord, which You Have Made for Your own dwelling, the sanctuary, O Lord, which Your Hands Have Established. 17 "The Lord shall Reign forever and ever." 18

"Now I know that The Lord is greater than all the gods; for in the very thing in which they behaved proudly, He was above them" (18:11). "When they have a difficulty, they come to Me, and I Judge between one and another; for I Make Known The Statutes of God and His Laws." 16 "Listen Now to My Voice; I will give you counsel, and God Will Be With You: Stand Before God for The People, so that you may bring the difficult to God. 19 And you shall teach them The Statutes and The Laws, and show them 'The Way' in which They Must Walk and The Work they must do." 20

Therefore let us pursue the things which makes for peace and the things by which One May Edify another (Rom. 14:19). Do you have faith? Have it to yourself before God. "Happy is he who does not condemn himself in what he approves." 22 For whatever things were written before were written for our learning, that we through The Patience of The Scriptures might have hope (15:4). But as it is written: "To whom He was not announced, they shall see; and those who have not heard shall understand." 21

"For I say to you, you shall see Me no more till you say, 'Blessed is He who comes in The Name of The Lord!'" (Matt. 23:39). "And unless Those Days were shortened, no flesh would be saved; but for 'The Elect's Sake' Those Days will be shortened" (24:22). "See, I have told you beforehand." 25 "And at midnight a cry was heard: 'Behold, The Bridegroom is Coming: go out to Meet Him!'" (25:6). "Assuredly, I Say to you, this generation will by no means pass away till all these things take place" (Mark 13:30). "For whoever is ashamed of Me and My Words, of him The Son of Man will be ashamed when 'He Comes in His Own Glory, and in His Father's, and of The Holy Angels" (Luke 9:26). "But I Tell You Truly, there are some standing here who shall not taste death till they see 'The Kingdom of God.'" 27

"He who hears you Hears Me, he who rejects you rejects Me, and he who rejects Me rejects Him Who Sent Me" (10:16). In That Hour Jesus Rejoiced in The Spirit and said, "I Thank You, Father, Lord of heaven and earth, that you have hidden These Things from the wise and prudent and revealed them to babes. Even so, Father, for so it seemed good in Your Sight." 21 "All Things have been delivered to Me by My Father, and no one knows who The Son is except The Father, and who The Father is except The Son, and The One to whom The Son 'Wills to Reveal Him.'" 22 "For I tell you that many prophets and kings have desired 'To See What You See,' and have not seen It, and 'To Hear What You Hear,' and have not heard It." 24 "Therefore Take Heed that The Light which is in you is not darkness" (11:35).

"For there is nothing covered that will not be revealed, nor hidden that will not be known" (12:2). Therefore whatever you have spoken in the dark will be heard in The Light, and what you have spoken in the ear in the inner rooms will be proclaimed on the housetops. 3 And I Say to you My Friends, be not afraid of those who kill the body, and after that have no more that they can do. 4 But I will show you whom you should fear: "Fear Him who, after He has killed, has power to cast into hell; yes, I Say to you, Fear Him!" 5

And He Said to them, "Take Heed and beware of covetousness, 'For One's Life does not consist in the abundance of the things he possesses.'"

15 "For all these things the nations of the world seek after, and Your Father Knows that you need these things." 30 "But Seek 'The Kingdom of God,' and all these things shall be added to you. 31 Do not fear, Little Flock, for it is Your Father's Good Pleasure to give you 'The Kingdom.'" 32

"These Things 'I Have Spoken' to you, that you should not stumble" (John 16:1). "They will put you out of the synagogues; yes, The Time is Coming that whoever kills you will think that he offers God service. 2 And these things they will do to you because they have not known The Father nor Me. 3 But These Things I have told you, that when the time comes, you may remember that I told you of them. And These Things I did not say to you at the beginning, because I Was With You. 4 These Things I have spoken to you in figurative language; but The Time is Coming when I will no longer speak to you in figurative language, but 'I Will Tell You' plainly about The Father." 25

Jesus spoke "These Words" lifted up His Eyes to heaven and said: "Father 'The Hour' has come. Glorify Your Son, that Your Son also may Glorify You" (John 17:1) "As You have given Him Authority over all flesh, that He Should Give 'Eternal Life' to as many as You Have Given Him. 2 And This Is Eternal Life, that They may Know You, The Only True God, and Jesus Christ Whom You Have Sent. 3 'I have Glorified You on the earth, I have finished 'The Work' which You have given Me to do.' 4 And now, O Father, Glorify Me together with Yourself, with The Glory which I had with You before the world was." 5

"I have manifested Your Name to the men whom You have given Me out of the world. They were Yours, You gave them to Me, and they have kept 'Your Word.' 6 Now they have known that All Things which You have given Me are from You. 7 For I have given to them 'The Words' which you have given Me; and they have received them, and have known surely that I Came Forth from You; and they have believed You Have Sent Me." 8

"I pray for them, I do not pray for the world but for those You Have Given Me, for they are Yours. 9 And all Mine are Yours, and Yours are Mine, and I Am Glorified in them. 10 Now I Am no longer in the world, but these are in the world, and I Come to You. Holy Father, keep through Your Name those whom You have given Me, that they be One as We Are. 11 While I was with them in the world, I kept them In Your Name. Those whom You gave Me I have kept; and none of them is lost except the son of perdition, that The Scripture might be fulfilled." 12

"But now I come to You, and These Things I speak in the world, that they may have My Joy fulfilled in themselves. 13 I have given them Your Word; and the world has hated them because they are not of the world, just as I Am not of the world. 14 I do not pray that You should take them out of the world, but that You should keep them from the evil one. 15 They are not of the world, just as I Am not of the world. 16 Sanctify them by Your Truth. 'Your Word is Truth.'" 17

"And You sent Me into the world, I also have sent them into the world. 18 And for their sake I Sanctify Myself, that they also may be Sanctified by The Truth. 19 I do not pray for these alone, but also for those who will Believe in Me through their word; 20 That they all may be One, as You, Father, are in Me, and I in You; that they also may be One in Us, that the world may believe that You Sent Me." 21

"And The Glory which You gave Me I have given them, that they may be One just as We are One: 22 I in them, and You in Me; that they may be made perfect in One, and that the world may know that You

Have Sent Me, and has loved them as You have loved Me. 23 Father, I desire that they also whom You Gave Me may be with Me where I Am, that They May Behold My Glory which You Have Given Me; for You Loved Me before the foundation of the world. 24 O Righteous Father! The world has not known You, but I have known You; and these have known that You Sent Me. 25 And I shave declared to them Your Name, and will declare It, that The Love with which You Loved Me may be in them, and I in them." 26

Now I saw heaven opened, and behold, A White Horse. And He who sat on him was called Faithful and True, and in righteousness He Judges and make war (Rev. 19:11). His eyes were like a flame of fire, and on His head were many crowns. He had "A Name" written that no one knew except Himself. 12 He was clothed with a robe dipped in blood, and His Name is Called "The Word of God." 13 And the armies in heaven, clothed in fine linen, white and clean, followed Him on white horses. 14 Now out of His mouth goes a sharp sword, that with it He should strike the nations. And He Himself will rule them with a rod of iron. He Himself treads the winepress of the fierceness and wrath of Almighty God. 15

"Thus says The Lord God: 'This is Jerusalem; I have set her in the midst of the nations and the countries all around her'" (Ezek. 5:5). She has rebelled against My Judgments by doing wickedness more than the nations, and against My Statutes more than the countries that are all around her; for they have refused My Judgments, and they have not walked in My Statutes. 6 "Therefore thus says The Lord God: 'Because you have multiplied disobedience more than the nations that are all around you, have not walked in My Statutes nor kept My Judgments, nor even done according to the judgments of the nations that are all around you.'" 7

"Therefore, as I Live," says The Lord God, "surely, because you have defiled My Sanctuary with all your detestable things and with all your abominations, therefore I will also diminish you; My Eye will not spare, nor will I have any pity." 11 "Thus shall My Anger be spent, I will cause My Fury to rest upon them, and I will be Avenged, and they shall know that I, The Lord, have spoken it in My Zeal, when I have spent My Fury upon them. 13 'So it shall be a reproach, a taunt, a lesson, and an astonishment to the nations that are all around you, when I execute judgments among you in anger and in fury and in furious rebukes,' I, The Lord, have spoken." 15

"Then those of you who escape Will Remember Me among the nations where they are carried captive, because I Was Crushed by their adulterous heart which has departed from Me, and by their eyes which play the harlot after their idols; they will loathe themselves for the evils which they have committed in all their abominations" (6:9). And they shall know that I Am The Lord; I have not said in vain that I would bring This Calamity upon them." 10 But if a man is just and does what is lawful and right (18:5). "If he has walked in My Statutes and kept My Judgments faithfully—he is just; he shall surely Live!" says The Lord God. 9 "You shall be My People, and I will be Your God" (Jer. 30:22). Behold, The Whirlwind of The Lord goes forth with fury, a continuing whirlwind; it will fall violently on the head of the wicked. 23 The Fierce Anger of The Lord will not return until He has done it, and until He has performed The Intent of His Heart. In "The Latter Days" you will consider it. 24

Be merciful to Me, O God, be merciful to Me! For My Soul trusts in You; and in The Shadow of Your Wings I will make My Refuge, until These Calamities have passed by (Ps. 57:1). I will cry out to God Most High, to God who performs all things for Me. 2 He shall send from heaven and Save Me; He reproaches the one who would swallow Me up. Selah. God shall send forth His Mercy and His Truth. 3 My soul is among lions; I lie among The Sons of Men who are set on fire, those teeth are spears and arrows, and their tongue a sharp sword. 4

Be Exalted, O God, above the heavens; let Your Glory be above all the earth. 5 They have prepared a net for My Steps; My soul is bowed down; they have dug a pit for Me; into the midst of it they themselves have fallen. Selah. 6 My heart is steadfast, O God, My heart is steadfast; I will sing and give praise. 7 Awake, My Glory! Awake, lute and harp! I will awaken the dawn. 8 I will Praise You, O Lord, among the peoples; I will sing to You among the nations. 9 For Your Mercy reaches unto the heavens, and Your Truth unto the clouds. 11 Be Exalted, O God, above the heavens; let Your Glory be above all the earth. 12

Those who make an image, all of them are useless, and their precious things shall not profit; they are their own witnesses; they neither see nor know, that they may be ashamed (Isa. 44:9). They do not know nor understand; for He has shut their eyes, so that they cannot see, and their hearts, so that they cannot understand. 18 He feeds on ashes; a deceived heart has turned him aside; and he cannot deliver his soul, nor say, "Is there not a lie in my right hand? 20 They shall be ashamed and also disgraced, all of them; they shall go in confusion together, who are makers of idols" (45:16).

This is A Faithful Saying: for if we died with Him, we shall also Live with Him (2 Tim. 2:11). If we endure, we shall also Reign with Him. If we deny Him, He also will deny us. 12 If we are faithless, He remains faithful; He cannot deny Himself. 13 Remind them of These Things, charging them Before The Lord not to strive about words to no profit, to the ruin of the hearers. 14 Be diligent to present yourself approved to

God, a worker who does not need to be ashamed, "Rightly Dividing" The Word of Truth. 15

In The Beginning was The Word, and The Word was with God, and The Word was God (John 1:1). He was in The Beginning with God. 2 All things were made through Him, and without Him nothing was made that was made. 3 In Him was Life, and "The Life" was The Light of Men. 4 And "The Light" shines in the darkness, and the darkness did not comprehend It. 5 And The Word became flesh and dwelt among us, and We beheld His Glory, The Glory as of The Only Begotten of The Father, "Full of Grace and Truth." 14

For you have said, "My Doctrine is Pure, and I Am clean in your eyes" (Job 11:4). But oh, that God would speak, and open His Lips against you. 5 That He would show you The Secrets of Wisdom! For they would double your prudence. Know therefore that God exacts from you less than your iniquity deserves. 6 Can you search out The Deep Things of God? Can you find out The Limits of The Almighty? 7 They are higher than heaven—What can you do? Deeper than Sheol—What can you know? 8 For He knows deceitful men; He sees wickedness also. Will He not consider it? 11

"If you would prepare your heart, and stretch out your hands toward Him; 13 If iniquity were in your hand, and you put it far away, and would not let wickedness dwell in your tents; 14 Then surely you could lift up your face without spot; yes, you could be steadfast, and not fear; 15 Because you would forget your misery, and remember it as waters that have passed away, 16 And 'Your Life' would be brighter then noonday. Though you were dark, you would be like the morning. 17 And you would be secure, because there is Hope; yes, you would dig around you, and 'Take Your Rest' safely." 18

"But now ask the beast, and they will teach you; and the birds of the air, and they will tell you" (12:7). Or speak to the earth, and it will teach you; and the fish of the sea will explain to you. 8 Who among all these does not know that The Hand of The Lord has done This, 9 In whose hand is "The Life" of every living thing, and The Breath of All Mankind? 10 And The Lord God formed man of the dust of the ground, and breathed into his nostrils The Breath of Life; and man became A Living Being (Gen. 2:7). For to "This End" we both labor and suffer reproach, because We Trust in The Living God, who is The Savior of All Men, especially of Those Who Believe (1 Tim. 4:10).

That which was from The Beginning, which we have heard, which we have seen with our eyes, which we have looked upon, and our hands have handled, concerning The Word of Life (1 John 1:1). The Life was manifested, and we have seen, and bear witness, and declare to you that Eternal Life which was with The Father and was manifested to us. 2 That which we have seen and heard we declare to you, that you also may have fellowship with us; and Truly our fellowship is with The Father and His Son Jesus Christ. 3

Do not love the world or the things in the world. If anyone loves the world, The Love of The Father is not in him (2:15). For all that is in the world—the lust of the flesh, the lust of the eyes, and the pride of life—is not of The Father but is of the world. 16 And the world is passing away, and the lust of it; but he who does "The Will of God" abides forever. 17

If then you were raised with Christ, seek those things which are above, where Christ is, sitting at The Right Hand of God (Col. 3:1). Set your mind on things above, not on things on the earth. 2 When Christ "Who Is Our Life" appears, then you also will appear with Him in Glory. 4 Therefore put to death your members which are on the earth;

fornication, uncleanness, passion, evil desire, and covetousness, which is idolatry. 5 Because of these things The Wrath of God is coming upon the sons of disobedience. 6

Therefore, as The Elect of GOD, Holy and Beloved, put on tender mercies, kindness, humility, meekness, longsuffering; 12 Bearing with one another, and forgiving one another, if anyone has a complaint against another; even as Christ forgave you, so you also must do. 13 Let The Word of Christ dwell in you richly in All Wisdom, teaching and admonishing one another in Psalms and Hymns and Spiritual Songs, Singing with Grace in your hearts to The Lord. 16 And whatever you do In Word or Deed, do all in The Name of The Lord Jesus, Giving Thanks to God The Father through Him. 17

And whatever you do, do it heartily, as To The Lord and not to men, 23 Knowing that From The Lord you will receive The Reward of The Inheritance; for you serve The Lord Christ. 24 But he who does wrong will be Repaid for what he has done, and there is no partiality. 25 But if you show partiality, you commit sin, and are convicted by The Law as transgressors (James 2:9). Let us search out and examine our ways, and Turn Back to The Lord (Lam. 3:40).

Blessed is he whose transgression is forgiven, whose sin is covered (Ps. 32:1). Blessed is the man to whom The Lord does not impute iniquity, and in whose spirit there is no deceit. 2 When I kept silent, my bones grew old through my groaning all day long. 3 For Day and Night Your Hand was heavy upon me; my vitality was turned into the drought of summer. Selah 4

I acknowledged my sin to You, and my iniquity I have not hidden. I said, "I will confess my transgressions to The Lord," and You forgive the iniquity of my sin. Selah 5 For "This Cause" everyone who is godly shall pray to You in a time when You may be found; surely in a flood of great waters they shall not come near to him. 6 You are my hiding place; You shall preserve me from trouble; You shall surround me with songs of deliverance. Selah 7

I will Instruct You and Teach You in "The Way" you should go; I will guide you with My Eye. 8 Do not be like the horse or like the mule, which has no understanding, which must be harnessed with bit and bridle, else they will not come near you. 9 Many sorrows shall be to the wicked; but he who Trusts in The Lord, mercy shall surround him. 10 Be Glad in The Lord and Rejoice; and shout for joy, all you Upright in Heart. 11

Blow the trumpet in Zion, and sound an alarm in My Holy Mountain! Let all the inhabitants of the land tremble; for The Day of The Lord is coming, for it is at hand (Joel 2:1). A day of darkness and gloominess, a day of clouds and thick darkness, like the morning clouds spread over the mountains. A people come, great and strong, the like of whom has never been; nor will there ever be any such after them, even for many successive generations. 2 A fire devours before them, and behind them a flame burns; the land is like The Garden of Eden before them, and behind them a desolate wilderness; surely nothing shall escape them. 3 The earth quakes before them, the heavens tremble; the sun and the moon grow dark, and the stars diminish their brightness. 10 The Lord gives Voice before His Army, for His camp is very great; for Strong is The One who executes His Word. For The Day of The Lord is great and very terrible; who can endure it? 11

Gather the people, sanctify the congregation, assemble the elders, gather the children and nursing babes; let The Bridegroom go out from his chamber; and The Bride from her dressing room. 16 "The Son of Man will send out His Angels, and they will gather out of His Kingdom all thing that offend, and those who practice lawlessness" (Matt. 13:41). "And will cast them into the furnace of fire. There will be wailing and gnashing of teeth. 42 Then The Righteous will shine forth as the sun in The Kingdom of Their Father. He who has ears to hear, let him hear!" 43

"For in 'Those Days' there will be tribulation, such as have not been since The Beginning of The Creation which God created until 'This Time,' nor ever shall be" (Mark 13:19). "And unless The Lord had shortened 'Those Days,' no flesh would be saved; but for The Elect's Sake, whom He Chose, He Shortened The Days. 20 But Take Heed; See, I have Told You All Things Beforehand. 23 And what I say to you, I say to all: WATCH!" 37

"But you do not believe, because you are not of My Sheep, as I said to you" (John 10:26). "My Sheep hear 'My Voice,' and I know them, and they Follow Me. 27 And I give them Eternal Life, and they shall never perish; neither shall anyone snatch them out of My Hand." 28 "And whoever Lives and Believes in Me shall never die. Do you believe This?" (11:26). Jesus answered and said, "This Voice did not come because of Me, but for Your Sake" (12:30). "Now is The Judgment of This World; now the ruler of this world will be cast out. 31 And I, if I Am lifted up from the earth, Will Draw All Peoples To Myself." 32

But although He had done so many signs before them, they did not believe in Him (12:37). That The Word of Isaiah the prophet might be fulfilled, which he spoke: "Lord, who has believed our report? And to whom has The Arm of The Lord been Revealed?" 38 Therefore they could not believe, because Isaiah said again: 39 "He has blinded their eyes and hardened their hearts, lest they should see with their eyes, lest they should understand with their hearts and 'Turn,' so that I Should Heal Them." 40 "He who rejects Me, and does not receive My Words, has that which judges him—The Word that I have spoken will judge him in The Last Day." 48

"Do you not believe that I Am in The Father, and The Father in Me? The Words that I speak to you I do not speak on My own authority; but The Father who dwells in Me 'Does The Works'" (14:10). "The Spirit of Truth, whom the word cannot receive, because it neither see Him nor knows Him; but you know Him, for He dwells with you and will be in you." 17 "But 'The Helper,' The Holy Spirit, whom The Father will send in My Name, He will teach you all things, and bring to your remembrance all things that I said to you." 26

"For Moses truly said to the fathers, 'The Lord your God will raise up for you A Prophet Like Me from Your Brethren. Him shall you hear in all things, whatever He says to do'" (Acts 3:22). "And it shall be that every soul who will not hear that Prophet shall be utterly destroyed from among The People." 23 "Yes, and all the Prophets, from Samuel and those who follow, as many as have spoken, have also foretold 'These Days.'" 24

"You are The Sons of The Prophets, and of The Covenant which God made with our fathers, saying to Abraham, 'And in Your Seed all The Families of The Earth shall be blessed.' 25 To you first, God, having raised up His Servant Jesus, sent Him to bless you, in turning away every one of you from your iniquities." 26 It is a fearful thing to fall into The Hands of The Living God (Heb. 10:31). For yet a little while, and He Who is Coming will come and will not tarry. 37 "And at midnight a cry was heard: 'Behold, The Bridegroom is Coming; go out to meet Him!'"

Give The King Your Judgments, O God, and Your Righteousness to The King's Son (Ps. 72:1). He will judge Your People with righteousness and Your poor with justice. 2 The Mountains will bring peace to the people, and the little hills, by righteousness. 3 He will bring justice to the poor of the people; He will save the children of the needy, and will break in pieces the oppressor. 4

In "His Days" the righteous shall flourish, and abundance of peace, until the moon is no more. 7 He shall have dominion also from sea to sea, and from The River to The Ends of The Earth. 8 His Name shall endure forever; His Name shall continue as long as the sun. And men shall be blessed in Him; all nations shall call Him Blessed. 17 Blessed be The Lord God, The God of Israel, who only does wondrous things! 18 And blessed be His Glorious Name forever! and let The Whole Earth be filled with His Glory. Amen and Amen. 19

And I said: "I Pray, Lord God of Heaven, O Great and Awesome God, You who keep Your Covenant and Mercy with those who love You and observe Your Commandments (Neh. 1:5). "Please let You Ear be attentive and Your Eyes open, that You May Hear The Prayer of Your Servant which I pray before You now, day and night, for The Children of Israel Your Servants, and confess the sins of The Children of Israel which we have sinned against You. Both my father's house and I have sinned. 6 We have acted very corruptly against You, and have not kept The Commandments, The Statutes, nor The Ordinances which You commanded Your Servant Moses." 7

"Remember, I Pray, The Word that You commanded Your Servant Moses, saying, 'If you are unfaithful, I will scatter you among the nations; 8 But if you Return to Me, and keep My Commandments and do them, though some of you were cast out to the farthest part of the heavens, yet I will gather them from there, and bring them to The Place which I have chosen as A Dwelling for My Name.' 9 Now these are Your Servants and Your People, whom You have Redeemed by Your Great Power, and by Your Strong Hand." 10

"Yet now our flesh is as the flesh of our brethren, our children as their children; and indeed we are forcing our sons and our daughters to be slaves, and some of our daughters have been brought into slavery. Is it not in our power to Redeem Them, for other men have our land and vineyards" (5:5). After serious thought, I rebuked the nobles and rulers, and said to them, 'Each of you is exacting usury from his brother.'" So I called A Great Assembly against them. 7 And I said to them, "According to our ability we have redeemed our Jewish Brethren who were sold to the nations. Now indeed, will you even sell your brethren? Or should they be sold to us?" Then they were silenced and found nothing to say. 8 Then I said, "What you are doing is not good. Should you not walk in The Fear of Our God because of the reproach of the nations, our enemies?" 9

"But they and our fathers acted proudly, hardened their necks, and did not heed Your Commandments" (9:16). They refused to obey, and they were not mindful of Your Wonders that You did among them. But they hardened their necks, and in their rebellion they appointed a leader to return to their bondage. But You are God, ready to pardon, gracious and merciful, slow to anger, abundant in kindness, and did not forsake them. 17 You also gave Your Good Spirit to instruct them, and did not withhold Your Manna from their mouth, and gave them water for their thirst. 20

"Nevertheless they were disobedient and rebelled against You, cast Your Law behind their backs and killed Your Prophets, who testified against them to Turn Them to Yourself; and they worked great provocations. 26 Yet for many years You had patience with them, and testified against them by Your Spirit in Your Prophets. Yet they would not listen; therefore You gave them into the hand of the peoples of the lands. 30 However You Are Just in all that has befallen us; For You have dealt faithfully, but we have done wickedly. 33 Then I contended with the nobles of Judah, and said to them, 'What evil thing is this that you do, by which you profane The Sabbath Day?'" (13:17). "Did not your fathers do thus, and did not Our God bring all this disaster on us and on this city? Yet you bring added wrath on Israel by profaning The Sabbath." 18

O Lord, do not rebuke me in Your Wrath, nor chasten me in Your Hot Displeasure! (Ps. 38:1). For Your Arrows pierce me deeply, and Your Hand presses me down. 2 There is no soundness in my flesh because of Your Anger, nor any health in my bones because of my sin. 3 For my iniquities have gone over my head; like a heavy burden they are too heavy for me. 4 My wounds are foul and festering because of my foolishness. 5 I am troubled, I am bowed down greatly; I go mourning all day long. 6 For my loins are full of inflammation, and there is no soundness in my flesh. 7 I am feeble and severely broken; I groan because of the turmoil of my heart. 8

Lord, all my desire is before You; and my sighing is not hidden from You. 9 My heart pants, my strength fails me; as The Light of My Eyes, it also has gone from me. 10 My loved ones and my friends stand aloof from my plague. and my relatives stand afar off. 11 Those also who seek

My Life lay snares for me; those who seek my hurt speak of destruction, and plan deception all day long. 12 But I, like a deaf man, do not hear; and I am like a mute who does not open his mouth. 13 Thus I AM like a man who does not hear, and in whose mouth is no response. 14

For in You, O Lord, I hope; You will hear, O Lord My God. 15 For I said, "Hear Me, lest they rejoice over me, lest, when my foot slips, they exalts themselves against me." 16 For I Am ready to fall, and my sorrow is continually before me. 17 For I will declare my iniquity; I will be in anguish over my sin. 18 But my enemies are vigorous, and they are strong; and those who hate me wrongfully have multiplied. 19 Those also who render evil for good, they are my adversaries, Because I Follow What Is Good. 20 Do not forsake me, O Lord; O My God, be not far from me! 21 Make haste to help me, O Lord, My Salvation! 22

Come Near, You Nations, to Hear; and heed, you people! Let the earth hear, and all that is in it, the world and all things that come forth from it (Isa. 34:1). For The Indignation of The Lord is against all nations, and His Fury against all their armies; He has utterly destroyed them, He has given them over to the slaughter. 2 "So I sought for a man among them who would make a wall, and stand in the gap before Me on behalf of the land, that I should not destroy it; but I found no one" (Ezek. 22:30). "Therefore I have poured out My Indignation on them; I have consumed them with The Fire of My Wrath; and I have recompensed their deeds on their own heads." says The Lord God. 31

"Behold! My Servant whom I have Chosen, My Beloved in whom My Soul is well pleased! I will put My Spirit upon Him, and He will declare justice to the Gentiles" (Matt. 12:18). He will not quarrel nor cry out, nor will anyone hear His Voice in the streets. 19 A bruised reed He will not break, and smoking flax He will not quench, till He Send Forth

Justice to Victory; 20 And in His Name Gentiles will trust." 21 And all the multitudes were amazed and said, "Could This be The Son of David?" 23

Why do the nations rage, and the people plot a vain thing? (Ps. 2:1). The kings of the earth set themselves, and the rulers take counsel together, against The Lord and against His Anointed, saying, 2 "Let us break their bonds in pieces and cast away their cords from us." 3 "I will declare The Decree: The Lord has said to Me, You are My Son, today I Have Begotten You. 7 Ask of Me, and I will give You the nations for Your Inheritance, and the ends of the earth for Your Possession. 8 You shall break them with A Rod of Iron; You shall dash them to pieces like A Potter's Vessel.'" 9

Now therefore, be wise, O kings; be instructed, you judges of the earth. 10 Serve The Lord with fear, and rejoice with trembling. 11 Kiss The Son, lest He be angry, and you perish in The Way, when His Wrath is kindled but a little. Blessed are all those who Put Their Trust in Him. 12 And He said to Me, "Do not seal The Words of The Prophesy of This Book, for The Time is at hand" (Rev. 22:10). And Behold, I Am coming quickly, and My Reward is with Me, to give to every one according to his work. 12 The Grace of Our Lord Jesus Christ be with you all. Amen. 21